ANTHONY SLY obtained [his degree at the Univer]sity of Reading and has [taught in several] Hertfordshire schools and co[lleges. Now head of] the Mathematics Department at Queen's School, Bushey, Herts, he is also a mathematics examiner and author of *A Short History of Computing* (Hertfordshire County Council Advisory Unit for Computer-based Education) and Key Facts *GCE O-level Passbook: Modern Mathematics*.

Model Answers

BIOLOGY, R. Whitaker, B.Sc., and J. M. Kelly, B.Sc.

CHEMISTRY, C. W. Lapham, M.Sc.

ENGLISH LANGUAGE, Keith Linley, M.A.

FRENCH, G. Butler, B.A.

GEOGRAPHY, R. Knowles, M.A.

HISTORY (*Social and Economic*, 1815–1939), M. C. James, B.A.

PHYSICS, D. F. Erskine, B.Sc.

As illustrations of both good and poor work, genuine student answers to examination questions have been included in each book in the *Model Answers* series. These student answers, which may contain errors, have been placed inside boxes wherever they occur, to distinguish them from the main body of the text.

Key Facts Model Answers

Modern
Mathematics

A. J. Sly, B.A.

Published by Intercontinental Book Productions
in conjunction with Seymour Press Ltd.
Distributed by Seymour Press Ltd.,
334 Bixton Road, London, SW9 7AG

Published 1977 by Intercontinental Book Productions,
Berkshire House, Queen Street, Maidenhead, Berks., SL6 1NF
in conjunction with Seymour Press Ltd.

1st edition, 1st impression 9.77.i.
Copyright © 1977 Intercontinental Book Productions
Made and printed by C. Nicholls & Company Ltd
ISBN 0 85047 910 X

Contents

Introduction:
Preparing for the examination

The most recent papers from all the GCE O-level examinations have been used to compile this book. Actual questions have been reproduced where permission has been given by the Boards concerned but all the other questions are modelled very closely on those that appear in the papers. The order of the topics follows that in the *GCE O-level Passbook: Modern Mathematics*. There is no direct reference to that book, but methods are explained more fully in it and it contains further model answers. The different examining Boards produce papers and questions of varying style and content, so we have attempted to provide different types of questions from those appearing in the *Passbook*, in order to give as wide a selection as possible.

The majority of examinations contain two papers, and the general pattern is a Paper I or Section A containing a large number of short answer or multiple choice questions, followed by a Paper II or Section B with fewer but longer questions. By setting a large number of the short answer questions the Boards are able to test most parts of the syllabus, so you would be unwise to concentrate on certain topics at the expense of others.

To ensure that you are completely familiar with the style of paper you are going to sit eventually, you are advised to obtain copies of the recent past papers of the Board concerned. The addresses are given on page 192 of the *Passbook*. The papers can also be ordered from a local bookshop.

To obtain maximum marks for a question it is necessary to show all essential working with your answer. The short answer questions often have to be answered concisely in the limited space provided on the answer paper. The use of a slide rule and, in some cases, an electronic calculator have made it virtually impossible to award many marks for calculations, so 'essential working' is inclined to mean now that the method should be clearly expressed. This book is intended to show you how to do this in such a way that the examiner is in no doubt of your intentions.

If you are competent in basic algebra and arithmetic your revision will be made easier. So many topics depend on these two that it is worthwhile starting with them. Practise solving equations, manipulating formulae and substituting numbers for letters. If you are going to use a slide rule to make calculations, practise with the one you intend to use in the examination until you are an expert. If you are permitted to use an electronic calculator, practise with it until you are completely confident in its use. Make sure that you can round off the answer it will give you. There are sure to be too many figures there.

A mathematics examination usually tests the ability to (i) remember factual knowledge, (ii) carry out mathematical manipulation, (iii) solve routine problems, (iv) understand mathematical ideas, (v) apply these to unusual problems and situations. As you revise keep these points in mind. Go through the topic thoroughly, learning basic formulae and terminology. Now turn to the questions on the topic in this book to see how they should be answered. To obtain the necessary practice, attempt the questions from the recent papers, saving one complete examination to the end to act as a trial against the clock. The timing of questions is important. It does vary with the style of paper, but as you practise your papers you will probably discover that the short answer questions vary from two to five minutes each and the longer answers will take between twenty to thirty minutes each depending on the Board involved.

When confronted with your actual examination read the instructions through carefully, noting the number of questions to be answered and the time allowed for the examination. Usually all of the short answer questions have to be attempted. Tackle them in order but do not spend too long on a question if you are finding some difficulty. Return to it later when a fresh start often produces new ideas. Do read each question right through before attempting an answer. Sometimes an important instruction is included in the last line. In the longer question section you will be given a choice of questions. Read the complete section through before attempting any answers. You will no doubt have some stronger topics which will tend to score higher marks, so attempt these questions first.

Finally do not leave your revision to the last moment. You are more likely to improve and overcome difficulties with regular practice.

Model Answers

Algebra

Sets

1. $\mathscr{E} = \{x : x \text{ a digit}\}$, $A = \{x : 3 \leqslant x < 8\}$
$B = \{x : x \geqslant 5\}$, $C = \{x : 2x + 1 = 7\}$
(i) *List the set $A' \cup B$.* (ii) *What is $n(A \cap B)'$?* (iii) *List the set C.*

Model answer
$\mathscr{E} = \{0, 1, 2, 3, 4, 5, 6, 7, 8, 9\}$ $A = \{3, 4, 5, 6, 7\}$ $B = \{5, 6, 7, 8, 9\}$
$A' = \{0, 1, 2, 8, 9\}$ $B' = \{0, 1, 2, 3, 4\}$

(i) $A' \cup B = \{0, 1, 2, 5, 6, 7, 8, 9\}$
(ii) $A \cap B' = \{3, 4\}$ $n(A \cap B') = 2$
(iii) $2x + 1 = 7 \Leftrightarrow 2x = 6$
       $\Leftrightarrow x = 3 \therefore C = \{3\}$.

Method To answer this question it is helpful to list first the elements of the sets involved. A' and B', the complements of A and B, contain the elements not in A and B respectively. (i) requires the elements in A' or B or both. (ii) requires the number of elements in A and B'. (iii) asks for the solution of the equation $2x + 1 = 7$.

2. If $\mathscr{E} = \{dogs\}$ $G = \{greedy\ dogs\}$
       $H = \{hungry\ dogs\}$ $F = \{fierce\ dogs\}$
Write the following statements in set notation, using any of the

9

symbols: $\cup, \cap, \subset, ', \neq, \emptyset$.

(a) *All greedy dogs are hungry.*
(b) *Some hungry dogs are not fierce.*
(c) *All hungry dogs are greedy and fierce.*
(d) *All fierce dogs are either greedy or hungry or both.*

Model answer

(a) $G \subset H$ (b) $H \cap F' \neq \emptyset$
(c) $H \subset (G \cap F)$ (d) $F \subset (G \cup H)$

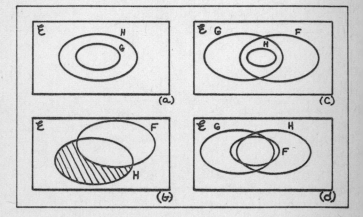

Method These questions are best answered with the help of Venn diagrams as shown above. Draw each one on the answer paper as an aid to forming the answers. (a) shows G as a subset of H. (b) shows the intersection of H and F'. This is not an empty set. (c) shows that H is a subset of the intersection of G and F. (d) shows that F is a subset of the union of G and H.

3. *A survey of 150 people shows that 85 of them read a daily paper, 67 read a Sunday paper, 45 read a weekly paper. Of those who read a daily, 9 read a weekly but not a Sunday, 20 read a Sunday but not a weekly, while 6 read both a Sunday and a weekly. 4 do not read any paper.*

Let x represent the number of people who only read a weekly paper and draw a Venn diagram to show this information.

How many people read
  (i) *a weekly and a Sunday but not a daily;*
 (ii) *one paper only;*
(iii) *two papers only?*

Model answer

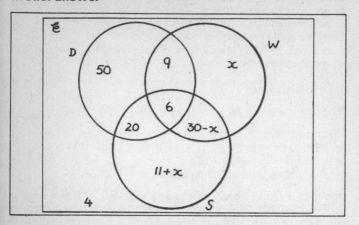

$n(\mathscr{E}) = 150$ $n(D \cap W \cap S') = 9$
$n(D) = 85$ $n(D \cap S \cap W') = 20$
$n(S) = 67$ $n(D \cap S \cap W) = 6$
$n(W) = 45$ $n(D' \cap S' \cap W') = 4$

Let $n(W \cap S' \cap D') = x$
then $n(S \cap W \cap D') = 45 - (15 + x) = 30 - x$
and $n(S \cap W' \cap D') = 67 - (20 + 6 + 30 - x)$
$\qquad\qquad\qquad\quad = 67 - (56 - x) = 11 + x$
$n(\mathscr{E}) = 150 = 50 + 9 + 6 + 20 + x + 30 - x + 11 + x + 4$
$\qquad \Leftrightarrow 150 = x + 85 + 45$
$\qquad \Leftrightarrow 150 = x + 130$
$\qquad \Leftrightarrow x = 150 - 130 \Leftrightarrow x = 20.$

(i) $n(W \cap S \cap D') = 30 - 20 = 10.$
(ii) Those who read one paper only $= 50 + x + 11 + x$
$\qquad\qquad\qquad\qquad\qquad\qquad = 50 + 20 + 11 + 20 = 101.$
(iii) Those who read two papers $= 9 + (30 - x) + 20$
$\qquad\qquad\qquad\qquad\qquad\qquad = 9 + 10 + 20 = 39$

Answers: (i) 10; (ii) 101; (iii) 39.

Method In the longer questions on sets write out the information given in set notation before preparing a clear Venn diagram. In the figure above, place the 6 in the area representing all three papers $(D \cap S \cap W)$, 9 in the area representing daily and weekly but not Sunday $(D \cap W \cap S')$ and 20 in the area representing daily and Sunday but not weekly $(D \cap S \cap W')$.
$n(D) = 85$ ∴ the remainder of D is $85 - (6 + 9 + 20) = 85 - 35 = 50.$

11

Now write down on the answer paper how the areas x, $30-x$, $11+x$ are obtained and place them on the diagram. The value of x must be found in order to answer the specific questions asked. Form the equation based on the fact that $n(\mathscr{E}) = 150$ and solve it to find that $x = 20$. Finally answer the questions showing clearly how each answer is obtained.

Basic algebra

4. *Find the common factor of $x^2 - 2x$ and $x^2 + 10x - 24$.*

Model answer
$$x^2 - 2x = x(x-2)$$
$$x^2 + 10x - 24 = (x-2)(x+12)$$
Answer: $(x-2)$ is the common factor.

Method Factorise both expressions, expecting to find a bracket common to both. Notice how the expressions are factorised. In the first a common factor of x is put outside a bracket and in the second the numbers inside the brackets are -2 and $+12$ because $-2 \times +12 = -24$ and $-2 + 12 = +10$.

5. *Simplify* $\dfrac{7}{x+2} - \dfrac{4}{x}$.

Model answer
$$= \frac{7x}{x(x+2)} - \frac{4(x+2)}{x(x+2)}$$

$$= \frac{7x - 4(x+2)}{x(x+2)}$$

$$= \frac{7x - 4x - 8}{x(x+2)}$$

Answer: $\dfrac{3x-8}{x(x+2)}$

Method Express each fraction in terms of the common denominator $x(x+2)$. Simplify the numerator, noting the signs when multiplying the bracket by -4.

6. *Solve the equation* $\frac{1}{3}x - \frac{1}{2}(x+2) = 2 \cdot 3$.

Model answer
$$\Leftrightarrow 10(\tfrac{1}{3}x - \tfrac{1}{2}(x+2)) = 10 \times 2 \cdot 3$$
$$\Leftrightarrow 2x - 5(x+2) = 23$$

$$\Leftrightarrow 2x - 5x - 10 = 23$$
$$\Leftrightarrow \quad -3x = 23 + 10$$
$$\Leftrightarrow \quad -3x = 33$$
$$\Leftrightarrow \quad x = \frac{33}{-3}$$

Answer: $x = -11$.

Method Multiply both sides of the equation by the common denominator 10. This removes the fractions, leaving a simple equation to solve.

7. $A = \{(x, y) : 4x + 3y = 9\}$ $B = \{(x, y) : 2x + 5y = 1\}$. *Calculate the values of x and y for which $(x, y) \in A \cap B$.*

Model answer

$4x + 3y = 9$ (i) $4x + 3y = 9$
$2x + 5y = 1$ (ii) $\times 2$ $4x + 10y = 2$

          subtracting $-7y = 7 \Leftrightarrow y = -1$

substitute in (ii) $2x - 5 = 1$
                $\Leftrightarrow 2x = 1 + 5$
                $\Leftrightarrow 2x = 6 \Leftrightarrow x = 3$

Answer: $x = 3$ $y = -1$.

Method Set A is the set of points on the straight line $4x + 3y = 9$; set B the points on the line $2x + 5y = 1$. $A \cap B$ is the point of intersection of the two lines, so this is a question about the solution of simultaneous equations. By multiplying equation (ii) by 2 the two x terms are the same. On subtraction they are eliminated to give $y = -1$. Substitute this value in either of the original equations, in this case (ii), to give $x = 3$.

8. *Solve the equations* (i) $3x^2 - 12 = 0$; (ii) $3x^2 - 12x = 0$; (iii) $3x^2 - 12x - 15 = 0$.

Model answer

(i) $3x^2 - 12 = 0 \Leftrightarrow 3(x^2 - 4) = 0$
                 $\Leftrightarrow 3(x - 2)(x + 2) = 0$
     $\Leftrightarrow$ either $x - 2 = 0$ or $x + 2 = 0 \Leftrightarrow x = \pm 2$

(ii) $3x^2 - 12x = 0 \Leftrightarrow 3x(x - 4) = 0$
     $\Leftrightarrow$ either $x = 0$ or $x - 4 = 0 \Leftrightarrow x = 0$ or   4

(iii) $3x^2 - 12x - 15 = 0 \Leftrightarrow 3(x^2 - 4x - 5) = 0$
           $\Leftrightarrow 3(x - 5)(x + 1) = 0$
     $\Leftrightarrow$ either $x - 5 = 0$ or $x + 1 = 0 \Leftrightarrow x = 5$ or -1

Answers: (i) $x = \pm 2$; (ii) $x = 0$ or   4; (iii) $x = 5$ or -1.

Method This question tests most methods of solving quadratic equations by factorising. In each case there is a common factor and the equations look so alike that it would be easy to become confused. In (i) take out the common factor of 3 to reveal the difference between two squares $x^2 - 4$. In (ii) there is a common factor of $3x$, leaving a simple factor in brackets. In (iii) the factorisation of the quadratic expression is simplified by taking out the common factor of 3 first. After factorising, to find the values of x use the argument that $ab = 0 \Leftrightarrow a = 0$ or $b = 0$.

9. *If* $y = \dfrac{x}{x+1}$ *express* x *in terms of* y.

Model answer

$$\Leftrightarrow y(x+1) = \frac{x(x+1)}{(x+1)}$$

$$\Leftrightarrow yx + y = x$$
$$\Leftrightarrow y = x - yx$$
$$\Leftrightarrow y = x(1-y) \quad \text{or} \quad x(1-y) = y$$
$$\Leftrightarrow \frac{x(1-y)}{(1-y)} = \frac{y}{1-y}$$
$$\Leftrightarrow x = \frac{y}{1-y}$$

Method There are x terms in the numerator and denominator. The aim is to isolate these terms on one side of the formula. To do this (i) multiply both sides of the formula by $(x+1)$ to eliminate the fraction. (ii) Multiply out the left-hand side. There are now no fractions or brackets so it is possible (iii) to rearrange the formula with the x terms on one side. (iv) This side now has a common factor of x, giving $x(1-y)$. (v) Divide both sides by $(1-y)$ to leave x on one side as the subject. Note that if x is to be the subject of the formula, the letter x must not appear on both sides of the formula.

10. $(x-4)^2 + (x-4)$ *is:* (A) $(x-4)(x-5)$ (B) $3(x-4)$
(C) $(x-4)(x-3)$ (D) $(x+5)(x-4)$

(C) is the correct answer.

Method This multiple choice question requires the factorisation of the given expression. $(x-4)$ is a bracket common to both terms. Taking out this factor the expression becomes:
$(x-4)((x-4)+1)$
$= (x-4)(x-3)$ which is the result (C).

Notice how a careless mistake at the last stage could make $-4+1$ equal to $+5$ or -5, producing results (A) or (D), both of which are incorrect.

11. $9x^2 - 18x + k$ *is to be a perfect square.* k *is the value:*
(A) -9 $\quad$ (B) $+81$ $\quad$ (C) -81 $\quad$ (D) $+9$

(D) is the correct answer.

Method $9x^2 - 18x + k$ will be in the form $(3x+A)^2$ where A is a number, if it is to be a perfect square.
$(3x+A)^2 = (3x+A)(3x+A) = 9x^2 + 6Ax + A^2$
Comparing this with the original expression:
$6Ax = -18x \qquad 6A = -18 \qquad A = -3$
$k = A^2 = (-3)^2 = +9$
(D) is the correct result.

Number systems and bases

12. $I = \{Integers\}$ $R = \{Rational\ numbers\}$ $N = \{Natural\ numbers\}$. *Copy and complete the table below, stating whether the numbers in the left-hand column are members of the sets* I, R, N. *Place a YES or NO in the appropriate place.*

	I	R	N
$1\cdot45$			
$\sqrt{1\cdot69}$			
$(\sqrt{2})^4$			
$(\sqrt{3}+1)^2$			

Model answer

	I	R	N
$1\cdot45$	NO	YES	NO
$\sqrt{1\cdot69}$	NO	YES	NO
$(\sqrt{2})^4$	YES	YES	YES
$(\sqrt{3}+1)^2$	NO	NO	NO

$I = \{\ldots -3, -2, -1, 0, 1, 2, 3, 4 \ldots\}$
$R = \{\frac{1}{2}, \frac{2}{3}, \frac{4}{3}, 0\cdot7, 1\cdot4, \frac{9}{4} \ldots\}$
$N = \{1, 2, 3, 4, 5, \ldots\}$

$\sqrt{1\cdot69} = 1\cdot3$

$$(\sqrt{2})^4 = \sqrt{2} \times \sqrt{2} \times \sqrt{2} \times \sqrt{2} = 2 \times 2 = 4$$
$$(\sqrt{3}+1)^2 = (\sqrt{3}+1)(\sqrt{3}+1) = 3 + 2\sqrt{3} + 1 = 4 + 2\sqrt{3}$$

Method Below the completed table show the working which was carried out in order to fill in the table.

$1 \cdot 45 = \frac{145}{100}$; $\sqrt{1 \cdot 69} = 1 \cdot 3 = \frac{13}{10}$. Both are fractions or ratios, $\therefore$ both belong to R but not to I or N.

$(\sqrt{2})^4 = 4$ which is a member of I, R and N.

When $(\sqrt{3}+1)^2$ is squared out the answer contains a $\sqrt{3}$ term which is irrational, $\therefore$ this number is not a member of I, R or N.

13. If $3x - 2y = 11$, *state any solution in negative integers.*

Model answer
Let $x = -1$, then $-3 - 2y = 11$
$-2y = 11 + 3 \qquad -2y = 14$
$\quad y = -7$
a solution is $x = -1 \qquad y = -7$

Method There are an infinite number of points on the straight line $3x - 2y = 11$. The aim is to find a point with coordinates which are negative integers. For this $-2y$ must be a positive even number, so $3x$ must be a negative odd number. This makes x any one of the values $-1, -3, -5, -7, -9 \ldots$.

14. $X = 321_5$, $Y = 2221_3$, $Z = 221_6$. *Write X, Y and Z in ascending order in base 2.*

Model answer

$X = 25$	5	1	$Y = 27$	9	3	1	$Z = 36$	6	1
	3	2	1		2	2	2	1	

$X = 25 \quad 5 \quad 1$
$\qquad\quad 3 \quad 2 \quad 1$
$= 75 + 10 + 1$
$= 86$

$Y = 27 \quad 9 \quad 3 \quad 1$
$\qquad\quad 2 \quad 2 \quad 2 \quad 1$
$= 54 + 18 + 6 + 1$
$= 79$

$Z = 36 \quad 6 \quad 1$
$\qquad\quad 2 \quad 2 \quad 1$
$= 72 + 12 + 1$
$= 85$

64	32	16	8	4	2	1	
1	0	0	1	1	1	1	79
1	0	1	0	1	0	1	85
1	0	1	0	1	1	0	86

Answer: $Y = 1001111$, $Z = 1010101$, $X = 1010110$.

Method Convert each number to base 10. Write down the column headings in each case. Then convert them into binary form, having put them into ascending order.

15. (a) If $56_7 + 43_7 = x_{10}$ *find the value of x.*
(b) *What is the largest three digit number that can be written in base 4? Write your answer as a denary number.*

Model answer

(a) $56_7 = 5 \times 7 + 6 \times 1 = 35 + 6 = 41$

   $43_7 = 4 \times 7 + 3 \times 1 = 28 + 3 = \underline{31}$

   Total $= \overline{\underline{72}}$

(b) Base 4   16   4   1

   largest number   3   3   3

   in base 10 $3 \times 16 + 3 \times 4 + 3 \times 1$

                  $= 48 + 12 + 3 = 63$

Answers (a) 72; (b) 63.

16. *If* $444_n + 555_n = 1221_n$ *the value of n is*

    (*A*) 4   (*B*) 5   (*C*) 9   (*D*) 8

(*D*) is the correct answer.

Method This question asks for the number base in which the sum is worked. In the units column $4 + 5 = 9$ in base 10, a 1 has been written down so 8 has been carried. This suggests the base is 8. Confirm this by carrying to the next column; hence (*D*) is correct.

Binary operations

17. *The operation * is defined as* $p * q = pq + 1$.

(*a*) *Calculate* (i) $(4 * 5) * 6$; (ii) $4 * (5 * 6)$.

(*b*) *Is the operation * associative? Give an example to show your answer.*

(*c*) *Give an example to show that the operation is commutative.*

(*d*) *Solve the equation* $9 * x = 3 * (x * 2)$.

Model answer

(a) (i) $4 * 5 = 4 \times 5 + 1 = 21$

      $(4 * 5) * 6 = 21 * 6 = 21 \times 6 + 1 = 126 + 1 = 127$

   (ii) $5 * 6 = 5 \times 6 + 1 = 30 + 1 = 31$

      $4 * (5 * 6) = 4 \times 31 + 1 = 124 + 1 = 125$

(b) The operation $*$ is not associative. Part (a) is an example, $(4 * 5) * 6 \neq 4 * (5 * 6)$.

(c) $4 * 5 = 21$ (from (a))

    $5 * 4 = 5 \times 4 + 1 = 21$

    $4 * 5 = 5 * 4$ is an example which shows that $*$ is commutative.

(d) $9 * x = 3 * (x * 2)$

    $\Leftrightarrow 9x + 1 = 3 * (2x + 1)$

    $\Leftrightarrow 9x + 1 = 3(2x + 1) + 1$

    $\Leftrightarrow 9x + 1 = 6x + 3 + 1$

    $\Leftrightarrow 9x - 6x = 3 + 1 - 1$

$$\Leftrightarrow 3x = 3 \Leftrightarrow x = 1$$

Answers: a (i) 127; (ii) 125; (b) NO. $(4*5)*6 \neq 4*(5*6)$; (c) $4*5 = 5*4$; (d) $x = 1$.

Method A binary operation is one which is carried out on two numbers. In this case it is $pq+1$. The associative law for $*$ is $(a*b)*c = a*(b*c)$ which is not true here. The commutative law is $a*b = b*a$ which is true here.

18. *The set $S = \{a, b, c, d, e, f,\}$ under the binary operation $*$, forms a group. The composition table for this group is shown here:*

$*$	a	b	c	d	e	f
a	c	f	a	e	d	b
b	f	e	b	c	a	d
c	a	b	c	d	e	f
d	e	c	d	f	b	a
e	d	a	e	b	f	c
f	b	d	f	a	c	e

(i) *What is the identity element of S under $*$? Give a reason for your answer.*

(ii) *State the inverse of each element of S.*

(iii) *How can you tell from the table that the operation is commutative?*

(iv) *Find x if $b*x = f*d$.*

(v) *Find a subset R of S with two elements and a subset T of S with three elements, such that R and T form groups under $*$. Draw up their composition tables.*

(The Associated Examining Board)

Model answer

(i) The identity element $= c$.

The identity element i of S under $*$ is such that $a*i = a$, $b*i = b$, $c*i = c$, etc. From the table $i = c$.

(ii) The inverse of a, a^{-1}, is such that $a*a^{-1} = c$.

$a^{-1} = a$ also $b^{-1} = d$

$c^{-1} = c$ $d^{-1} = b$

$e^{-1} = f$ $f^{-1} = e$.

(iii) The table is symmetrical about the diagonal through $*$, $\therefore$ $a*b = b*a$, $b*c = c*b$, etc., for all pairs of elements of S. Hence the operation is commutative.

(iv) $f*d = a$, $b*e = a \therefore x = e$.

(v) $R = \{a, c\}$

*	a	c
a	c	a
c	a	c

$T = \{c, e, f\}$

*	c	e	f
e	e	f	c
f	f	c	e

Method Study the given table to obtain the answers. Give reasons in complete sentences using the correct notation where possible. (i), (ii) and (iii) test a knowledge of the terms used in group work. (v) requires subsets R(two elements) and T(three elements) with the four group properties: closure, identity element, inverses and associativity. It is given that S is a group, so assume associativity, the identity element and inverses have been established, $\therefore$ search for subsets that are closed under $*$. $R = \{a, c\}$ and $T = \{c, e, f\}$ are the only possible sets.

Student answers

A student's answers to questions 1 and 7 are now reproduced.

1. $\mathscr{E} = \{0, 1, 2, 3, 4, 5, 6, 7, 8, 9\}$ $\qquad A' = \{0, 1, 2, 8, 9\}$
$A = \{3, 4, 5, 6, 7\}$ $\qquad\qquad\qquad B' = \{0, 1, 2, 3, 4\}$
$B = \{5, 6, 7, 8, 9\}$

(i) $A' \cup B = \{0, 1, 2, 5, 6, 7, 8, 9\}$; (ii) 3; (iii) $x = 3$.

The sets were listed correctly and (i) answered properly. (ii) is incorrect and there is no way of telling how the answer was obtained. (iii) gives the correct value of x, but the question asked for the set to be listed, so the answer should be in the form $C = \{3\}$. Again no working is shown. Marks could be deducted for this.

7. $\qquad 4x + 3y = 9$
$\qquad\quad 2x + 5y = 1$
$\qquad\quad 4x + 10y = 2$
$\Rightarrow \qquad -13y = 7 \Rightarrow y = -\frac{7}{13}$

$\Rightarrow 4x - 3 \times \dfrac{7}{13} = 9$

$\Rightarrow 4x - \dfrac{21}{13} = 9$

$$\Rightarrow 4x = 9 + \frac{21}{13} = \frac{117 + 21}{13} = \frac{138}{13}$$

$$x = \frac{138}{4 \times 13} = \frac{138}{52} = \frac{69}{26}$$

$$\therefore x = 2\tfrac{17}{26} \quad y = -\tfrac{7}{13}.$$

The student realised that the two equations must be solved simultaneously. The second equation has been doubled correctly, but in subtraction $-13y$ has appeared instead of $-7y$. From here the arithmetic has become difficult and time-consuming (compare this with the correct answer). A double check after finding the value of y might have found this error, especially as it is a rather unusual value!

Common errors

Perhaps the most common error is to enter the examination without a sound knowledge of the terms used in modern mathematics. For example, a candidate cannot answer question 1 without knowing the meaning of the word 'digit', even though the symbols $A' \cup B$ and $A \cap B'$ are well understood. Consider the question 'Solve the equation $x^2 - 5x - 14 = 0$, where x is a real number.' The inclusion of the term 'real number' did worry many candidates, who thought that there must be a trick somewhere. In fact the solutions 7 and -2 found by factorising are real numbers. It is the correct term used to described any number on the number line.

The short questions on sets are often well answered, but in the longer ones, like question 4, an early mistake occurs which makes it impossible to gain any marks. Look at the statement '85 people read a daily paper'. It is interpreted – incorrectly – as meaning that they *only* read a daily paper. In fact, the 85 include all those who read a daily and a Sunday; a daily and a weekly; a daily and a Sunday and a weekly. $n(D) = 85$ is the total of all the numbers in the balloon labelled D (see figure on page 11).

Questions are set to test the candidate's ability to write statements in set notation, e.g.: Simplify $P \cap Q$ if P and Q are such that $P \subset Q$.

The correct answer is $P \cap Q = P$ and not a short explanation in words like 'all of P is in Q'.

Several examinations have asked for a complete list of the subsets of the set $\{1, 2\}$. The correct answer contains 4 subsets, $\{1\}$, $\{2\}$, $\varnothing$, $\{1, 2\}$. The last two are often omitted. Remember that the empty set $\varnothing$ is a subset of every set, i.e. $\varnothing \subset A$, and any set is a subset of itself, i.e. $A \subset A$ or $A \cap A = A$.

Errors in basic algebra account for a large proportion of lost marks. Short questions are set to test basic techniques, but many of the long questions depend on accurate algebraic manipulation for a correct answer.

Consider (i) $\dfrac{a+b}{a}$ and (ii) $\dfrac{x-5}{x+10}$. It is not possible to cancel the a's in (i) or the x's in (ii), since there is no common factor in the numerator and the denominator, e.g. $\dfrac{a+ab}{a} = \dfrac{a(1+b)}{a} = 1+b$. The a's do cancel here. Similarly $\dfrac{(x-5)(x+10)}{x+10} = x-5$. The $(x+10)$'s cancel here.

Manipulation of quadratic expressions often causes difficulties: factorising and solving are confused. E.g. (i) factorise $x^2 - 3x - 4$ and (ii) solve $x^2 - 3x - 4 = 0$ have the following correct solutions:
(i) $x^2 - 3x - 4$
$\quad = (x-4)(x+1)$

(ii) $x^2 - 3x - 4 = 0$
$\quad \Leftrightarrow (x-4)(x+1) = 0$
$\quad \Leftrightarrow$ either $x - 4 = 0$ or $x + 1 = 0$
$\quad \Leftrightarrow x = 4$ or $\quad -1$

Notice that the factorising question has brackets in the answer but the solution requires the values of x which satisfy the equation. Furthermore take care about the signs in the brackets, here -4 and $+1$ because $-4 + 1 = -3$, and at the same time $-4 \times +1 = -4$.

The solutions of the following quadratic equations produce some predictable errors: (i) $x(x-3) = 10$; (ii) $x^2 = 4$; (iii) $x^2 = 4x$.

In (i) it is incorrect to say that $x = 10$ or $x - 3 = 10$. $ab = 10 \Leftrightarrow a = 10$ or $b = 10$ is a false argument. This has been confused with the correct one that $ab = 0 \Leftrightarrow a = 0$ or $b = 0$. To avoid this error start by making the right-hand side of the equation equal to 0 thus:
$x(x-3) - 10 = 0$
$\Leftrightarrow x^2 - 3x - 10 = 0 \qquad$ multiply out the bracket

$\Leftrightarrow (x-5)(x+2) = 0$ factorise the expression
$\Leftrightarrow$ either $x-5 = 0$ or $x+2 = 0$
$\Leftrightarrow x = 5$ or -2

In (ii) the solution $x = -2$ is often omitted. The square of -2 is also $+4$. In (iii) it is common to cancel off the x's leaving the single answer $x = 4$. Notice that $x = 0$ is also a solution. The correct solutions are as follows:

(ii) $x^2 = 4 \Leftrightarrow x = \pm 2$.

(iii) $x^2 = 4x$
$\qquad \Leftrightarrow x^2 - 4x = 0$
$\qquad \Leftrightarrow x(x-4) = 0 \Leftrightarrow x = 0$ or 4

Questions involving the rearrangement of formulae are always badly answered. Every possible algebraic error appears. There are usually two or more methods of obtaining the correct answer and this adds to the confusion rather than relieving it. Study the two methods of making d the subject of the formula $a = b + \dfrac{c}{d}$. Both are correct and they are followed by some of the errors that might occur.

(i) $\Leftrightarrow d \times a = d\left(b + \dfrac{c}{d}\right)$

$\qquad \Leftrightarrow da = db + c$

$\qquad \Leftrightarrow da - db = c$

$\qquad \Leftrightarrow d(a-b) = c$

$\qquad \Leftrightarrow d = \dfrac{c}{a-b}$

(ii) $\Leftrightarrow a - b = \dfrac{c}{d}$

$\qquad \Leftrightarrow \dfrac{1}{a-b} = \dfrac{d}{c}$

$\qquad \Leftrightarrow \dfrac{c}{a-b} = d$

In (i) the second line would produce $da = b + c$ if the candidate omits to multiply b by d. (ii) in the second line would read $\dfrac{1}{a} - \dfrac{1}{b} = \dfrac{d}{c}$, which is an incorrect inversion of fractions.

Briefly, other errors which occur regularly more through careless-ness than lack of knowledge are:

$3x = 4 \Leftrightarrow x = \frac{3}{4}$, which should be $x = \frac{4}{3}$.

$4(x + y) = 4x + y$, which should be $4x + 4y$.

$5x - 2(x + 3) = 5x - 2x + 6$, which should be $5x - 2x - 6$.

Check your working at intervals to see that no careless mistakes are spoiling your answer.

In number base work, errors can be reduced if the column headings are written down first. For example in base 4 the headings are ...256 64 16 4 1. An error can occur here if these headings are written ...16 *8* 4 1. The numbers must progress in powers of the base.

Functions and inequalities

Functions

9. f *and* g *are the functions* $f : x \rightarrow 4x - 1$ $g : x \rightarrow x^2 + 2$. *Find* (i) $f(2)$; (ii) $gf(3)$; (iii) fg.

Model answer
(i) $\quad f(2) = 4 \times 2 - 1 = 8 - 1 = 7$
(ii) $\quad f(3) = 4 \times 3 - 1 = 12 - 1 = 11$
$\quad\quad gf(3) = g(11) = 11^2 + 2 = 121 + 2 = 123$
(iii) $\quad fg = f(x^2 + 2) = 4(x^2 + 2) - 1$
$\quad\quad\quad\quad\quad\quad\quad = 4x^2 + 8 - 1$
$\quad\quad\quad\quad\quad\quad\quad = 4x^2 + 7$

Answers: (i) 7; (ii) 123; (iii) $4x^2 + 7$.

Method (i) $f : x \rightarrow 4x - 1$ can be written $f(x) = 4x - 1$. $f(2)$ means 'let $x = 2$ in f'. (ii) $gf(3)$ can be written $g(f(3))$. First put $x = 3$ in f and follow this by putting the result 11 for x in g. (iii) fg can be written $f(g(x))$ when no specific value of x is stated. In f write $x^2 + 2$ for x.

20. $f : x \rightarrow 4x + 5$ *and* $g : x \rightarrow \frac{1}{2}(1 + 3x)$. *Find* (i) f^{-1}; (ii) g^{-1}; (iii) $f^{-1}g^{-1}(2)$.

Model answer
(i)

take x $\longrightarrow$ $\boxed{\times 4}$ $\longrightarrow$ $\boxed{+5}$ $\longrightarrow$ $f(x) = 4x + 5$

$f^{-1}(x) = \dfrac{x - 5}{4}$ $\boxed{\div 4}$ $\longleftarrow$ $\boxed{-5}$ $\longleftarrow$ take x

(ii)

take x $\longrightarrow$ $\boxed{\times 3}$ $\longrightarrow$ $\boxed{+1}$ $\longrightarrow$ $\boxed{\div 2}$ $f(x) = \dfrac{3x + 1}{2}$

$g^{-1}(x) = \dfrac{2x - 1}{3}$ $\boxed{\div 3}$ $\longleftarrow$ $\boxed{-1}$ $\longleftarrow$ $\boxed{\times 2}$ take x

(iii)
$g^{-1}(2) = \dfrac{2 \times 2 - 1}{3} = \dfrac{4 - 1}{3} = 1$

$$f^{-1}(1) = \frac{1-5}{4} = \frac{-4}{4} = -1$$

Answers: (1) $f^{-1} = \dfrac{x-5}{4}$; (ii) $g^{-1} = \dfrac{2x-1}{3}$; (iii) -1.

Method (i) f^{-1} the inverse function of f is found by first making a flowchart for evaluating f for any value of x. Next form the flowchart which is the complete inverse starting from the right. The result on the left is f^{-1}. (ii) g^{-1} is found in a similar way. (iii) requires $x = 2$ in g^{-1} followed by this result for x in f^{-1}.

21. *A is the point $(0, -4)$ and B is the point $(5, 6)$. The straight line AB cuts the x axis at C. Find (i) the slope of AB; (ii) the equation of AB; (iii) the coordinates of C; (iv) length AB.*

Model answer

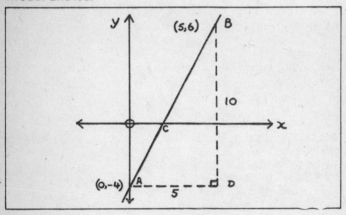

(i) The slope of $AB = \dfrac{6-(-4)}{5-0} = \dfrac{10}{5} = 2$

(ii) Let the line be $y = mx + c$
$m = 2$ and $c = -4$ $\therefore$ the line AB is $y = 2x - 4$

(iii) let $y = 0 \Leftrightarrow 0 = 2x - 4$
$\Leftrightarrow 4 = 2x \Leftrightarrow x = 2$
$\therefore C$ is the point $(2, 0)$

(iv) $AB^2 = 10^2 + 5^2$
$AB^2 = 100 + 25 = 125$
$\therefore AB = 11 \cdot 2$ units.

Method Draw a diagram for any question which involves coordinates (see the figure on page 25). Complete the right-angled triangle ABD. BD is 10 units and AD is 5 units. (i) The slope of a line $= \dfrac{\text{vertical}}{\text{horizontal}}$. (ii) $y = mx + c$ is the straight line with gradient m cutting the y axis at $(0, c)$. (iii) Any point on the x axis has its y coordinate equal to 0. (iv) Use the theorem of Pythagoras in triangle ABD.

22. *The sketch in the diagram represents part of the graph of the function $y = x^2 + ax + b$. (i) Find the values of a and b; (ii) list the set $\{x : x \text{ an integer}, y \leqslant 0\}$.*

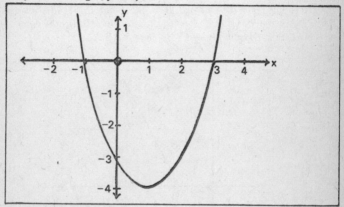

Model answer
(i) From the sketch, when $x = 0$, $y = -3$
$-3 = 0 + 0 + b \Leftrightarrow b = -3$.
The curve is now $y = x^2 + ax - 3$.
When $x = 3$ $y = 0 \Leftrightarrow 0 = 9 + ax - 3$
$\Leftrightarrow 0 = 6 + 3a$
$\Leftrightarrow 3a = -6 \Leftrightarrow a = -2.$
(ii) $y \leqslant 0$ in the range $-1 \leqslant x \leqslant 3$
$\therefore$ the required set $S = \{-1, 0, 1, 2, 3\}$.

Method (i) The value of the constant term b is the y coordinate of the point where the curve meets the y axis. To find a substitute another known point in the equation of the curve. Here $(3, 0)$ has been chosen. (ii) The region $y \leqslant 0$ is the part of the curve which lies below and on the x axis, i.e. $-1 \leqslant x \leqslant +3$, but the question requires the list of integer values of x only.

23. *The table shows the values of x and y which can be connected in particular ways.*

x	2	4	b
y	6	a	15

Find the values of (i) a, if y varies as the square of x; (ii) b, if y varies as the inverse of x.

Model answer

(i)
$$y = kx^2$$
$$x = 2, y = 6 \Rightarrow 6 = k \times 4$$
$$\Leftrightarrow k = \tfrac{6}{4} \text{ or } \tfrac{3}{2}$$
$$y = \tfrac{3}{2}x^2$$
$$\text{when } x = 4 \; y = \tfrac{3}{2} \times 16 = 3 \times 8$$
$$\therefore a = 24.$$

(ii)
$$y = \frac{k}{x}$$

$$x = 2, y = 6 \Rightarrow 6 = \frac{k}{2}$$

$$\Leftrightarrow k = 12$$

$$\Leftrightarrow y = \frac{12}{x}$$

$$y = 15 \Rightarrow 15 = \frac{12}{x} \Rightarrow x = \frac{12}{15} = \frac{4}{5}$$

$$\therefore b = 0 \cdot 8.$$

Method (i) Note how the relationship 'y varies as the square of x' is written. With $x = 2$, $y = 6$ given, it is possible to find the particular value of k and from there the value of a. (ii) is a similar process, but tests 'y varies as the inverse of x'.

24. At 1000 hrs a cyclist sets off from a town A to ride to a town B which is 30 km away. For the first $\tfrac{3}{4}$ hr he cycles at a steady speed of 16 km/hr. He then rests before completing the journey at 1300 hr at a steady speed of 14 km/hr. Using a scale of 4 cm to represent 1 hr and 1 cm to represent 2 km, draw the distance/time graph of the journey from A to B. For how many minutes did the cyclist rest? At 1200 hrs a lorry sets off from B to drive to A on the same road at a steady speed of 40 km/hr. At what time and how far from A does the lorry pass the cyclist?

Model answer

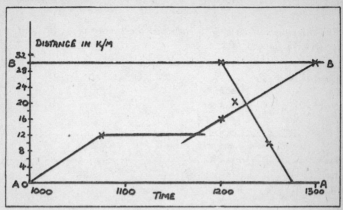

The cyclist rests between 1045 and 1143 hr,
∴ he rests for 58 minutes.
The lorry meets the cyclist at X;
The time = 1215 hrs approximately;
The distance from A = 19 km approximately.

Method On any graph involving time as a variable use the horizontal axis to measure time. Mark in the times and distances on the axes, keeping strictly to the scale given. Label the axes and the towns A and B as shown in the figure above. The cyclist travels 12 km in the first $\frac{3}{4}$ hr so mark in the point (1045, 12) and join to the origin. His rest period is shown by a horizontal line whose length is to be determined. The final stage is shown on the graph by joining the points (1200, 16) and (1300, 30) which represents 14 km/hr. Produce this line to meet the horizontal line. The length of the horizontal line determines the required time. The lorry's journey can be plotted by joining (1200, 30) to (1230, 10) to represent 40 km/hr. The point X where it crosses the cyclist's graph gives the required time and distance. Notice that the lorry starts at B and travels to A.

25. *The graph in the diagram shows the velocity/time graph for a train travelling at v m/s for t seconds. Find (i) the initial acceleration in m/s^2; (ii) for how long the train travelled at constant speed; (iii) the total distance travelled by the train.*

28

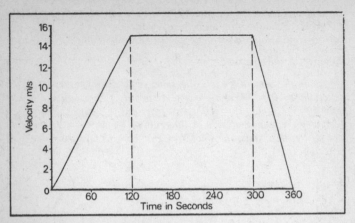

Model answer

(i) Acceleration $= \dfrac{15}{120} = \dfrac{1}{8}$ m/s^2.

(ii) The time for constant speed $= 300 - 120 = 180$ seconds.

(iii) The total distance travelled $=$
$(\frac{1}{2} \times 120 \times 15) + (180 \times 15) + (\frac{1}{2} \times 60 \times 15)$
$= (60 \times 15) + (180 \times 15) + (30 \times 15)$
$= 15(60 + 180 + 30)$
$= 15 \times 270$
the distance travelled $= 4050$ m.

Method (i) The gradient on a velocity/time graph measures the acceleration, $\therefore$ find the vertical:horizontal ratio. (ii) Constant speed appears as a horizontal line on the velocity/time graph. (iii) The total distance travelled is the total area under the velocity/time graph. In this case the area is divided conveniently into two triangles and one rectangle. Notice that a factor of 15 can be removed from the brackets in the calculation to facilitate the working.

26. *Copy and complete the table of values for the function* $y = \dfrac{x^2}{2} + \dfrac{12}{x} - 7$ *for values of x between 1 and 5.*

x	1	1·5	2	2·5	3	3·5	4	4·5	5
y		2·12		0·92		2·55		5·79	7·9

On graph paper, using a scale of 2 cm to 1 unit on each axis, draw the graph of the function in the given range.

(a) Use your graph to estimate (i) the minimum value of y; (ii) the solutions of the equation $\dfrac{x^2}{2} + \dfrac{12}{x} - 7 = 5$.

(b) Using the same axes and the same scale draw the graph of the function $y = 2 + x$. Write down and simplify the equation which is solved by the intersection of the two functions. Estimate the solutions.

(c) Using the trapezium rule at intervals of $\frac{1}{2}$ unit, estimate the area cut off by the x axis, the lines $x = 3$ and $x = 5$ and the curve $y = \dfrac{x^2}{2} + \dfrac{12}{x} - 7$.

Model answer

$x = 1 \qquad y = \frac{1}{2} + 12 - 7 = 5 \cdot 5$

$x = 2 \qquad y = \frac{4}{2} + 6 - 7 = 1$

$x = 3 \qquad y = \frac{9}{2} + 4 - 7 = 1 \cdot 5$

$x = 4 \qquad y = \frac{16}{2} + 3 - 7 = 4$

The completed table is:

x	1	1·5	2	2·5	3	3·5	4	4·5	5
y	5·5	2·12	1	0·92	1·5	2·55	4	5·79	7·9

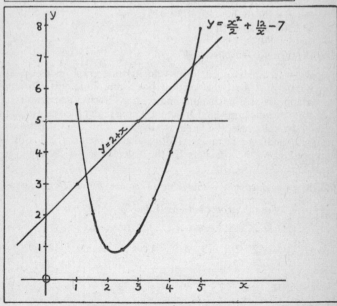

(a) (i) The minimum value of $y = 0.87$.

    (ii) The solutions are $x = 1$ and 4.3.

(b)

x	1	3	5
y	3	5	7

$$\frac{x^2}{2} + \frac{12}{x} - 7 = 2 + x$$

$$\Leftrightarrow x^3 + 24 - 14x = 4x + 2x^2$$

$$\Leftrightarrow x^3 + 24 - 14x - 4x - 2x^2 = 0$$

The required equation is $x^3 - 2x^2 - 18x + 24 = 0$.

The estimated solutions are $x = 1.3$ and 4.7.

(c) Area of trapezium $= \frac{1}{2}(a+b)h$. The area under the curve $=$
$\frac{1}{2}(1.5 + 2.55) \times \frac{1}{2} + \frac{1}{2}(2.55 + 4) \times \frac{1}{2} + \frac{1}{2}(4 + 5.79) \times \frac{1}{2} + \frac{1}{2}(5.79 + 7.9) \times \frac{1}{2}$
$= \frac{1}{4}(1.5 + 2.55 + 2.55 + 4 + 4 + 5.79 + 5.79 + 7.9)$
$= \frac{1}{4} \times 34.08$
the required area $= 8.5$ units^2.

Method To complete the table of values, make the necessary calculations on the answer paper. Note the ranges in the values of x and y, so that when the axes are drawn all the points can be plotted on the paper. Keeping strictly to the scale allotted, plot the points and join them in a clear, continuous curve.

(a) (i) The minimum value of y occurs between $x = 2$ and $x = 2.5$. Notice how the curve continues below the point $(2.5, 0.92)$ and the minimum value of y is approximately 0.86. (ii) Draw the line $y = 5$ on the graph and read off the values of x where it cuts the curve.

(b) $y = 2 + x$ is a straight line. Make a table to find the coordinates of three points, enough to plot a straight line accurately. The intersection of the line and curve solves the equation formed by equating the two functions. To simplify the equation multiply both sides by $2x$ to eliminate the fractions, then rearrange the terms into descending powers of x.

(c) The trapezium rule obtains an approximate value for the area by dividing it into a series of trapeziums with equal bases, in this case $\frac{1}{2}$ unit. The lengths of the parallel sides are the values of y when $x = 3, 3.5, 4, 4.5, 5$ and are found in the table of values.

Inequalities

27. (a) *Express* $1 - \frac{5}{4}x > \frac{3}{2}(x - 12)$ *as simply as possible. State the largest integer* x *which satisfies the equation.* (b) *Find the solution set of the inequality* $(2x - 3)(x + 3) \leqslant 0$ (i) *where the members are from* *the set of integers, and (ii) where the members are from the set of real numbers.*

Model answer

(a) $1 - \frac{5}{4}x > \frac{3}{2}(x-12)$

$\Leftrightarrow 4(1-\frac{5}{4}x) > 4 \times \frac{3}{2}(x-12)$

$\Leftrightarrow 4-5x > 6x-72$

$\Leftrightarrow -5x-6x > -72-4$

$\Leftrightarrow -11x > -76 \Leftrightarrow 11x < 76$

The simplest form is $x < \frac{76}{11}$.

The greatest integer x is 6.

(b) Consider $y = (2x-3)(x+3)$

When $x = 0$, $y = (-3)(+3) = -9$;

When $y = 0$ $\qquad (2x-3)(x+3) = 0$

$\qquad\qquad\qquad\qquad \Leftrightarrow x = 1.5 \quad \text{or} \quad -3$

The curve passes through the points $(-3, 0)$ $(0, -9)$ $(1.5, 0)$.

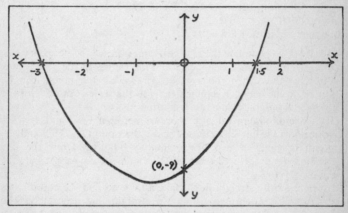

(i) $y \leqslant 0$ for the integers $\{-3, -2, -1, 0, 1\}$

(ii) $y \leqslant 0$ for the real numbers $-3 \leqslant x \leqslant 1.5$.

Method (a) Solve the inequation by multiplying both sides by 4 to eliminate the fractions. Rearrange the terms to find that both sides are negative. Remember to reverse the arrow when changing the signs. $\frac{76}{11} = 6\frac{10}{11}$ ∴ the largest possible integer is 6. In (b) the function is quadratic and the method used here is to sketch the curve which will be a parabola. It is sufficient to find where it cuts the x axis ($y = 0$) and the y axis ($x = 0$) and sketch the general shape as shown in the figure above. Answer (i) lists the integers in the range $-3 \leqslant x \leqslant 1.5$. For answer (ii) if x is real then x is any number on the number line in the range $-3 \leqslant x \leqslant 1.5$.

28. *On a single diagram on squared paper shade in the region defined by* $x + y \geqslant 7$; $5x + 12y \geqslant 60$; $x \leqslant 5$; $y < 6$. *State the coordinates of the point* (x, y) *which give* (i) *the greatest value of* $2x + y$; (ii) *the greatest value of* $2x - y$, *where* x *and* y *are integers.*

Model answer

$x + y = 7$ when $x = 0$, $y = 7$ when $y = 0$, $x = 7$
the line cuts the axes at $(7, 0)$ and $(0, 7)$.

$5x + 12y = 60$ when $x = 0$ $12y = 60$ $y = 5$
                      when $y = 0$ $5x = 60$ $x = 12$
the line cuts the axes at $(12, 0)$ and $(0, 5)$.

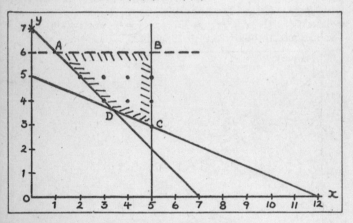

The integer values (x, y) in the region ABCD are:
$(2, 5)$ $(3, 4)$ $(3, 5)$ $(4, 4)$ $(4, 5)$ $(5, 3)$ $(5, 4)$ $(5, 5)$.
(i) The point $(5, 5)$ gives the maximum $2x + y$;
(ii) The point $(5, 3)$ gives the maximum $2x - y$.

Method To plot the straight lines $x + y = 7$ and $5x + 12y = 60$, find their intercepts with the axes by putting $x = 0$ and $y = 0$. Draw them and $x = 5$ followed by $y = 6$ in a broken line. Shade in the areas above $x + y = 7$, $5x + 12y = 60$, to the left of $x = 5$ and below $y = 6$. ABCD is the required area – excluding the line AB. List the integer points (x, y) to find that the greatest $2x + y$ requires the greatest x and y and the greatest $2x - y$ requires the greatest x with the least y possible.

29. *A householder has 28 electric sockets in his home which are suitable for table lamps. Two types of table lamps are available – 60 watt and 40 watt. 60 watt table lamps cost £6 each and 40 watt* *table lamps cost £4·50 each. The total sum of money available for purchasing table lamps is £150. If x 60 watt and y 40 watt are bought and used, write down two linear constraints on x and y, in addition to the constraints $x \geqslant 0$, $y \geqslant 0$. All lamps purchased must be used. Show the constraints on a linear programming diagram, and determine the maximum total wattage which may be achieved by a suitable choice of x and y.*

(Southern Universities Joint Board)

Model answer

The constraints are: $x + y \leqslant 28$ $6x + 4 \cdot 5y \leqslant 150$.

If $x + y = 28$ $x = 0$ $y = 28$ and $y = 0$ $x = 28$

If $6x + 4 \cdot 5y = 150 \Leftrightarrow 12x + 9y = 300$

$\Leftrightarrow 4x + 3y = 100$ $x = 0$ $y = 33\frac{1}{3}$: $y = 0$ $4x = 100 \Leftrightarrow x = 25$

The lines pass through $(28, 0)$ $(0, 28)$ and $(25, 0)$ $(0, 33\frac{1}{3})$.

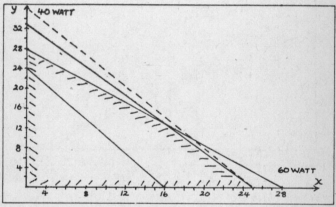

The total wattage $W = 60x + 40y$

Plot the line $60x + 40y = 960$

$x = 0$, $y = 24$; $y = 0$, $x = 16$

The maximum value of W occurs when $60x + 40y = W$ passes through the point $(25, 0)$ when $W = 60 \times 25 + 0$

∴ the maximum wattage = 1500 watts.

Method Form the inequalities as shown. Simplify $6x + 4 \cdot 5y \geqslant 150$ to $12x + 9y \leqslant 300$, ready for plotting the straight lines as shown in question 28. $x \geqslant 0$ and $y \geqslant 0$ denotes the use of the positive axes only. The total wattage $60x + 40y = W$ is a straight line graph. Take any value of W (960 makes the calculation simpler) and plot the graph. Place a set square against the line and move it parallel until it reaches the extremity of the permitted region furthest from the origin, in this case at $(25, 0)$ (shown as a broken line). Hence $x = 25$ and $y = 0$ gives the maximum wattage possible.

Student answers

A student's answer to question 26 is now reproduced.

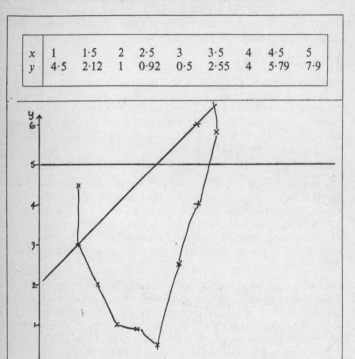

x	1	1·5	2	2·5	3	3·5	4	4·5	5
y	4·5	2·12	1	0·92	0·5	2·55	4	5·79	7·9

(a) (i) minimum $y = 0·5$
    (ii) $x = 4·3$

(b) $\dfrac{x^2}{2} + \dfrac{12}{x} - 7 = 2 + x$

    $x = 1·2$ and $4·5$

(c) area of trapezium =

The table of values contains two incorrect values of y and there is no working shown. Consequently the shape of the graph is incorrect, the minimum inaccurate and the solutions to a (ii) incomplete. Careless placing of the axes has made it impossible to plot $(5, 7\cdot9)$ and neither graph is labelled. In (ii) the correct equation has been formed but it has not been simplified. (c) cannot be attempted because the area formula is not known. This student should have realised that the shape of the curve is unusual and checked his working to find the errors.

Common errors

Algebraic errors often occur in this section, in particular the substitution of numbers for letters. E.g. if $y = 9 - x^2$ and $x = -2$ the correct answer is $9 - (-2)^2 = 9 - (+4) = 5$ and not $9 + 4 = 13$. Also if $y = 3x^2$ and $y = (3x^2)$ when $x = 4$ the correct values are
$y = 3x^2 = 3 \times 4^2 = 3 \times 16 = 48$
$y = (3x)^2 = (3 \times 4)^2 = 12^2 = 144$.
There is often confusion between these two expressions.

The function questions $f : x \rightarrow$ often require such numerical substitution and in this context there is confusion between domain and range. Remember that the domain maps onto the range, e.g. if $f : x \rightarrow 2x$ then the domain $\{1, 2, 3, 4\}$ maps onto the range $\{2, 4, 6, 8\}$. The compound function $f(g(x))$ is manipulated in the order $g(x)$ followed by f (as in the product of transformations work from right to left).

Sketches of graphs are often too rough and lacking in information. They should be clear, give a good idea of the shape of the curve and contain any necessary information, e.g. coordinates of points where the curve cuts the axes. See the figure on page 32. Drawings of accurate graphs on graph paper also suffer from lack of care. Errors in the table of values will cause the shape of the curve to be wrong. Careless joining up of points causes inaccuracies in solutions of equations and inequalities. Always use the scale given and pay particular attention to the measurement of gradients if the scales on the x and y axes differ, e.g. the line $y = x$ is only at $45°$ to the x axis if the scales on the x and y axes are the same.

The use of the straight line equation $y = mx + c$ is often faulty, e.g. the gradient of the straight line $3x + 4y = 7$ is not $+3$ or -3 as often appears. It is necessary to rearrange the equation as follows:
$\Leftrightarrow 4y = -3x + 7$
$\Leftrightarrow y = -\frac{3}{4}x + \frac{7}{4}$
giving the gradient $m = -\frac{3}{4}$ and the intercept with the y axis $(0, \frac{7}{4})$.

Note also that a line or curve cuts the y axis where $x = 0$ and the x axis where $y = 0$, which often causes confusion.

Study questions 24 and 25 to see that on the distance/time graph the gradient measures the velocity – a horizontal line denotes that the object is at rest. On the velocity/time graph the gradient measures the acceleration. A horizontal line denotes a constant velocity. These points are often confused. In this context the formula

distance = velocity × time

can only be used when the velocity is constant. To find the distance travelled when the velocity varies, calculate the area under the velocity/time graph. To calculate the average speed of a journey use the formula

$$\text{average speed} = \frac{\text{total distance}}{\text{total time}}.$$

In question 24 the total distance = 30 km, the total time = 3 hr ∴ the average speed is $30 \div 3 = 10$ km/hr. It is incorrect to take the the average of the two speeds 14 and 16 km/hr.

The main fault in inequality questions is that candidates resort to guesswork. In question 27 (b) it takes the construction of a sketch to see the correct range. Using guesswork, answers could vary from $x = \frac{3}{2}$ or -3 to $x > \frac{3}{2}$ or $x < -3$, but without some substantiating calculation they gain no marks. The main source of error in the manipulation of inequalities occurs when both sides are multiplied by a negative number. The arrow must be reversed if the statement is to remain true, e.g. $-x > -4 \Leftrightarrow x < 4$.

Graph work associated with inequalities provokes the complaints already listed above, and indicates difficulties over the following points. With reference to question 28, the line $y = 6$ is a horizontal line, $x = 5$ is vertical. The region $x + y > 7$ lies above the line $x + y = 7$; the region $x + y < 7$ would lie below that line. The shading of these areas often becomes too heavy, making it impossible to read off any information accurately. By shading the relevant area adjacent to the line it is possible to see the required region and still read off any points. See figures on pages 33 and 34.

Geometry and vectors

Geometry

30. *AD is a diameter of a circle centre O. A chord BC intersects AD at X and the tangent at D at a point E, so that angle BED = 32°. Angle BCD = 84°. Calculate (i) angle DXC; (ii) angle ABX; (iii) angle BOD.*

Model answer

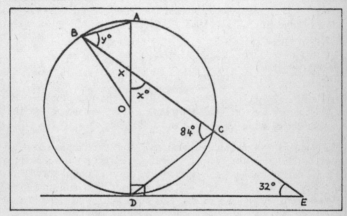

 (i) angle $ADE = 90°$ (radius and tangent)
 in triangle XDE $x° = 180 - (90 + 32) = 180 - 122$
 $$x = 58°.$$
 (ii) angle $BAX = 84°$ (angle on the same chord)
 angle $BXA = 58°$ (vertically opposite)
 in triangle BAX $y° = 180 - (84 + 58) = 180 - 142$
 $$y = 38°$$
(iii) angle $BOD = 2 \times 84° = 168°$ (the angle at the centre)
Answers: (i) angle $DXC = 58°$; (ii) angle $ABX = 38°$; (iii) angle $BOD = 168°$.

Method It is not easy to draw a neat diagram straight off, so make a rough sketch first to obtain the general idea. (i) The theorem used is: a radius and the tangent at the point of contact are at right angles. (ii) The theorem used is: the angles subtended at the circumference by an arc are equal. (iii) The theorem used is: the angle which an arc subtends at the centre of a circle is twice the angle it subtends at the circumference.

31. *ABCD is a square. P is a point on AB, and Q is a point on CD such that AP = CQ = $\frac{1}{3}$AB. The diagonal AC cuts PD at X and BQ at Y. (i) What shape is BQDP (no proof required)?*
(ii) Prove that triangle APX and triangle ABY are similar.

(iii) *Calculate* $\dfrac{XY}{AX}$ *and* $\dfrac{BY}{PX}$ *(no proof required).*

(iv) *Calculate* $\dfrac{area\ PBQD}{area\ ABCD}$ *(no proof required).*

(v) *Calculate* $\dfrac{area\ APX}{area\ ABCD}$ *(no proof required).*

(Southern Universities Joint Board)

Model answer

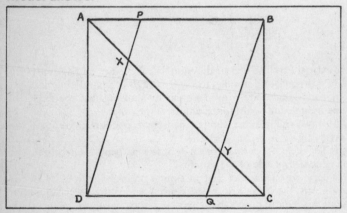

(i) *BQDP* is a parallelogram.

(ii) In triangles *APX* and *ABY*
  XP is parallel to *BY*
  ∴ angle *APX = ABY* and angle *AXP = AYB* (corresponding angles)
  angle *XAP* is common to both triangles
  ∴ triangles *APX* and *ABY* are similar (the angles of each are equal).

(iii) $\dfrac{AX}{AY} = \dfrac{PX}{BY} = \dfrac{AP}{AB} = \dfrac{1}{3}$
  $AX = \frac{1}{3}AY \Rightarrow XY = \frac{2}{3}AY$
  $XY = \frac{2}{3} \times 3\,AX \Rightarrow XY = 2\,AX$

39

$$\Rightarrow \frac{XY}{AX} = \frac{2}{1} \quad \text{and} \quad \frac{BY}{PX} = \frac{3}{1}.$$

(iv) Area $PBQD = DQ \times AD = PB \times AD$
$\qquad\qquad\qquad = \frac{2}{3} AB \times AD$
$AB \times AD = $ area of $ABCD$

$$\therefore \frac{\text{area } PBQD}{\text{area } ABCD} = \frac{2}{3}.$$

(v) Area APX : area $AYB = 1:9$
area APX : area $PXYB = 1:8$
area $PXYB = \frac{1}{2}$ area $PDQB$
$\therefore$ area $PXYB = \frac{1}{2} \times \frac{2}{3} ABCD = \frac{1}{3} ABCD$
$8 \times$ area $APX = \frac{1}{3} ABCD$

$$\Rightarrow \frac{\text{area } APX}{\text{area } ABCD} = \frac{1}{24}.$$

Method Produce a clear diagram like the figure on page 39.
(i) PB is equal and parallel to DQ $\therefore$ $PBQD$ is a parallelogram.
(ii) The triangles are proved similar by showing that the angles of one triangle are equal to the angles of the other.
(iii) If two triangles are similar their corresponding sides are in the same ratio.
(iv) The area of a parallelogram = base × perpendicular height. The height AD is a side of the square.
(v) depends on the fact that in similar triangles with sides in the ratio $1:n$, the areas are in the ratio $1:n^2$. Although the question does not require proofs, basic working must be shown.

32. (x, y) *is a point such that* $x \neq y$. $R(x, y)$ *is the rotation of* (x, y) *about* $(0, 0)$ *through* $90°$ *anticlockwise.* $M(x, y)$ *is the reflection of* (x, y) *in the x axis. Which of the following are true and which are false?*
(i) $MR(x, y)$ *is equivalent to the reflection of* (x, y) *in the line* $y = -x$.
(ii) $MR(x, y)$ *is equivalent to the rotation of* (x, y) *about* $(0, 0)$ *through* $90°$ *clockwise followed by a reflection in the y axis.*
(iii) $MR(x, y) = RM(x, y)$
(iv) $M(x, y)$ *is equivalent to giving* (x, y) *a half turn about* $(0, 0)$ *followed by a reflection in the y axis.*

Model answer

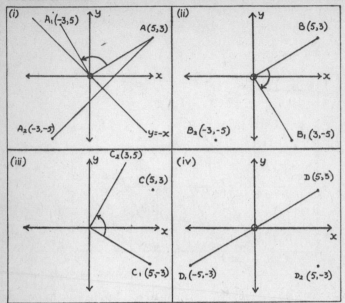

(i) TRUE; (ii) TRUE; (iii) FALSE; (iv) TRUE.

Method To answer this question draw four sketches applying each transformation to a particular point, say $(5, 3)$. (i) requires transformation R followed by M. Under R, $A \to A_1$ followed by M in which $A_1 \to A_2(-3, -5)$, the same result obtained when reflecting $(5, 3)$ in $y = -x$, $\therefore$ the statement is true. (ii) Renaming the point B $(5, 3)$, under the rotation of $90°$ clockwise $B \to B_1$ followed by a reflection in the y axis $B_1 \to B_2(-3, -5)$, $\therefore$ this statement is true. (iii) Renaming the point C, RM requires M followed by R. M gives $C \to C_1$ followed by R gives $C_1 \to C_2(3, 5)$, $\therefore$ the statement is false. (iv) Renaming the point D, under a half turn $D \to D_1$ followed by a reflection in the y axis $D_1 \to D_2(5, -3)$. Under M directly $D \to D_2(5, -3)$, $\therefore$ this statement is true.

33. *On squared paper plot the rectangle with vertices $A(0, 4)$, $B(4, 4)$, $C(4, 10)$, $D(0, 10)$.*
(i) *$ABCD$ is mapped onto $A_1B_1C_1D_1$ by a reflection in the line $y = x$. Find the coordinates of $A_1B_1C_1D_1$.*
(ii) *$A_1B_1C_1D_1$ is sheared onto $A_1B_2C_2D_1$ so that $B_1 \to B_2(6, 4)$. Find the coordinates of C_2.*

41

(iii) $A_1B_2C_2D_1$ is mapped onto $A_2B_3C_3D_2$ by an enlargement with centre $(0,0)$ and scale factor $1\cdot5$. Find the coordinates of $A_2B_3C_3D_2$. (iv) Calculate the area of $A_2B_3C_3D_2$.

Model answer

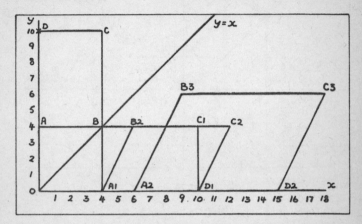

(i) $A_1 = (4,0)$, $B_1 = (4,4)$, $C_1 = (10,4)$, $D_1 = (10,0)$.
(ii) $C_2 = (12,4)$.
(iii) $A_2 = (6,0)$, $B_3 = (9,6)$, $C_3 = (18,6)$, $D_2 = (15,0)$.
(iv) Area $= 9 \times 6 = 54$ units^2.

Method Using a generous scale plot the points A, B, C, D and the line $y = x$. Plot A_1 so that A and A_1 are equidistant from $y = x$ and on opposite sides of it. The line AA_1 is perpendicular to $y = x$. Repeat this process to find $B_1C_1D_1$, noting that B stays at $(4,4)$, i.e. B is invariant. (ii) B_1 $(4,4) \rightarrow B_2(6,4)$ provides a shear of $+2$ units parallel to the x axis; $\therefore$ $C_1 \rightarrow C_2(12,4)$. Notice that A_1 and D_1 are invariant. (iii) For an enlargement in $(0,0)$ of scale factor $1\cdot5$ the distance $OA_2 = 1\frac{1}{2} \times OA_1$, $\therefore$ A_2 is at $(6,0)$; similarly D_2 is at $(15,0)$. To obtain $OB_3 = 1\frac{1}{2} \times OB_2$ notice that B_2 is a corner of a rectangle 6 units by 4 units, $\therefore$ B_3 will be at the corresponding corner of a rectangle 9 units by 6 units, i.e. B_3 is the point $(9,6)$. C_3 is found in a similar way. (iv) The area of a parallelogram = base $\times$ perpendicular height.

34. The point $P(4,5)$ is mapped onto P_1 by a rotation of $90°$ anticlockwise about the centre $(2,1)$. P_1 is mapped onto P_2 by a translation $\binom{-2}{-5}$. Find the coordinates of P_2.

42

Model answer

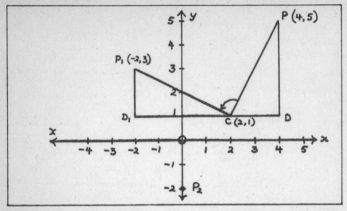

P_2 is the point $(0, -2)$.

Method This time the rotation is not about the origin. To find the point P_1 plot the points $(4, 5)$, the centre $(2, 1)$ and join them. The angle $P_1 CP$ is to be 90° and $PC = P_1 C$. To obtain these complete the right-angled triangle PDC to find that $PD = 4$ units and $CD = 2$ units. Now measure $CD_1 = 4$ units horizontally to the left, followed by 2 units vertically upwards to the required point P. A translation of $(-\frac{2}{3})$ means: go 2 units → parallel to the x axis followed by 5 units ↓ parallel to the y axis.

Vectors

A reminder: a **vectors** quantity possesses both **magnitude** and **direction**. The pilot of a small aircraft must know the direction of the wind as well as its speed if he is to plot his course correctly, e.g. 30 km/hr from due south. This tells him the **velocity** of the wind. Velocity is a vector. It requires both magnitude and direction. Notice that the speed of the wind is the magnitude of the velocity. Force and displacement are other examples of vector quantities. In print vectors are generally shown in bold type, **a**, or, where direction is not specified, $\vec{AB}$. Indicate vectors in your work by underlining— $\underline{a}$ or $\underline{a}$.

35. (a) A triangle OAB has $\vec{OA} = \mathbf{a}$, $\vec{OB} = \mathbf{b}$. Point D is taken on AB such that $AD = \frac{2}{3} AB$. Express $\vec{AB}$ and $\vec{OD}$ in terms of $\mathbf{a}$ and $\mathbf{b}$. (b) If $\mathbf{c} = 8\mathbf{i} + 15\mathbf{j}$, calculate (i) the length of $\mathbf{c}$; (ii) the gradient of $\mathbf{c}$; (iii) the angle which $\mathbf{c}$ makes with the horizontal.

Model answer

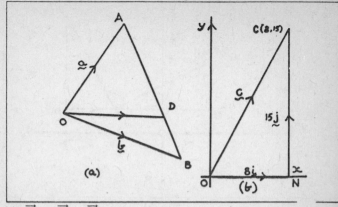

(a)

(b)

(a) $\vec{AB} = \vec{AO} + \vec{OB}$
$= -\mathbf{a} + \mathbf{b} \;\therefore\; \vec{AB} = \mathbf{b} - \mathbf{a}$
in triangle OAD $\vec{OD} = \vec{OA} + \vec{AD} = \vec{OA} + \frac{2}{3}\vec{AB}$
$= \mathbf{a} + \frac{2}{3}(\mathbf{b} - \mathbf{a})$
$\vec{OD} = \frac{1}{3}\mathbf{a} + \frac{2}{3}\mathbf{b}$.

(b) (i) the length of $\mathbf{c} = OC = \sqrt{(8^2 + 15^2)}$
$= \sqrt{(64 + 225)} = \sqrt{289}$
$\therefore OC = 17$ units.

(ii) The gradient of $\mathbf{c} = \frac{15}{8}$.

(iii) $\tan CON = \frac{15}{8} = 1\cdot875$
the required angle $= 61\cdot9°$.

Method (a) This is a test of basic vector manipulation. Draw the triangle OAB as in the figure above marking in $\mathbf{a}$ and $\mathbf{b}$ with their directional arrows. To find $\vec{AB}$ write down the vector addition $\vec{AB} = \vec{AO} + \vec{OB}$ using the capital letters of the triangle. In the next line change this to $\mathbf{a}$'s and $\mathbf{b}$'s (noting that $\vec{AO} = -\mathbf{a}$). $\vec{OD}$ is found in a similar way using the fact that $AD = \frac{2}{3}AB$ gives $\vec{AD} = \frac{2}{3}\vec{AB}$. (b) $\mathbf{i}$ and $\mathbf{j}$ are unit vectors along the x and y axes respectively. Draw the axes and mark in the point $C(8,15)$. (i) Use the theorem of Pythagoras in triangle CON to find the length of $\mathbf{c}$. (ii) The gradient is measured by the ratio $\dfrac{\text{vertical}}{\text{horizontal}}$. (iii) The gradient of $\mathbf{c}$ is the tangent of the angle CON.

36. $\mathbf{a} = \begin{pmatrix} 2 \\ 5 \end{pmatrix}$ $\mathbf{b} = \begin{pmatrix} 3 \\ -1 \end{pmatrix}$ $\mathbf{c} = \begin{pmatrix} 3 \\ 16 \end{pmatrix}$

Find (i) $\mathbf{a} + \mathbf{b}$; (ii) *the values of* p *and* q *if* $p\mathbf{a} + q\mathbf{b} = \mathbf{c}$.

Model answer

(i)
$$\mathbf{a} + \mathbf{b} = \begin{pmatrix} 2 \\ 5 \end{pmatrix} + \begin{pmatrix} 3 \\ -1 \end{pmatrix} = \begin{pmatrix} 5 \\ 4 \end{pmatrix}.$$

(ii)
$$p \begin{pmatrix} 2 \\ 5 \end{pmatrix} + q \begin{pmatrix} 3 \\ -1 \end{pmatrix} = \begin{pmatrix} 3 \\ 16 \end{pmatrix}$$

$$\Leftrightarrow \begin{pmatrix} 2p \\ 5p \end{pmatrix} + \begin{pmatrix} 3q \\ -q \end{pmatrix} = \begin{pmatrix} 3 \\ 16 \end{pmatrix}$$

$\Leftrightarrow$ (i) $2p + 3q = 3 \Leftrightarrow 2p + 3q = 3$
(ii) $5p - q = 16 \Leftrightarrow 15p - 3q = 48$

$$\text{adding} \Rightarrow 17p = 51$$
$$\Leftrightarrow p = \tfrac{51}{17} = 3$$

substitute in (ii) $5 \times 3 - q = 16$
$\Leftrightarrow q = 15 - 16 = -1$
$\therefore p = 3$ and $q = -1$.

Method (i) Vectors **a** and **b** are written in column form. **a** signifies a displacement of $2 \rightarrow$ followed by a displacement of $5 \uparrow$. To find **a** + **b** add the corresponding displacements. (ii) p and q are scalars. To find them, form two simultaneous equations and solve them.

37.

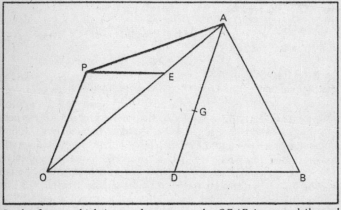

In the figure, which is not drawn to scale, OPAB is a quadrilateral with D the mid-point of OB, E is on OA such that $OE = 2EA$, G is on DA such that $2DG = GA$, PE is parallel to OB and $PE = \frac{1}{3}OB$. If $\vec{OA} = 6\,\mathbf{a}$ and $\vec{OB} = 6\,\mathbf{b}$ write down the following in terms of **a** and **b**: (i) $\vec{DA}$ (ii) $\vec{DG}$ (iii) $\vec{OG}$ (iv) $\vec{PA}$. Prove OGAP is a parallelogram.

(Welsh Joint Education Committee)

45

Model answer

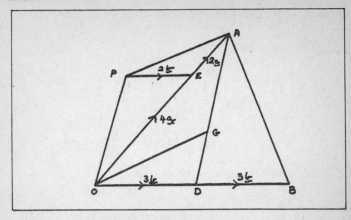

$\vec{OD} = \vec{DB} = 3\,\mathbf{b}$ $\vec{PE} = 2\,\mathbf{b}$

$OE : EA = 2 : 1$ $\therefore$ $\vec{OE} = 4\,\mathbf{a}$ $\vec{EA} = 2\,\mathbf{a}$.

(i) In triangle OAD $\vec{DA} = \vec{DO} + \vec{OA}$

$\qquad\qquad\qquad\qquad = -3\,\mathbf{b} + 6\,\mathbf{a}$ $\therefore$ $\vec{DA} = 6\,\mathbf{a} - 3\,\mathbf{b}$.

(ii) $DG : GA = 1 : 2$ $\therefore$ $\vec{DG} = \frac{1}{3}\vec{DA}$

$\quad \vec{DG} = \frac{1}{3}(6\,\mathbf{a} - 3\,\mathbf{b})$ $\therefore$ $\vec{DG} = 2\,\mathbf{a} - \mathbf{b}$

(iii) In triangle OGD $\vec{OG} = \vec{OD} + \vec{DG}$

$\qquad\qquad\qquad\qquad = 3\,\mathbf{b} + 2\,\mathbf{a} - \mathbf{b}$ $\therefore$ $\vec{OG} = 2\,\mathbf{a} + 2\,\mathbf{b}$

(iv) In triangle PEA $\vec{PA} = \vec{PE} + \vec{EA}$

$\qquad\qquad\qquad\qquad = 2\,\mathbf{b} + 2\,\mathbf{a}$ $\therefore$ $\vec{PA} = 2\,\mathbf{a} + 2\,\mathbf{b}$

$\qquad \therefore\ \vec{PA} = \vec{OG}$

PA is equal and parallel to OG, $\therefore$ $OGAP$ is a parallelogram.

Method Make a copy of the diagram and interpret the information given in vector form, e.g. $OE = 2\,EA$ means that $OE = \frac{2}{3}OA$ and $\vec{OE} = 4\,\mathbf{a}$. Mark this and the other vectors obtained on the diagram, as illustrated in the figure above, showing the arrows clearly. Now attempt to express $\vec{DA}$ and $\vec{DG}$ in terms of $\mathbf{a}$ and $\mathbf{b}$. (i) $\vec{DA}$ can be found by forming the vector addition in triangle ODA in which $\vec{OD}$ and $\vec{OA}$ are known vectors in terms of $\mathbf{a}$ and $\mathbf{b}$. (ii) $\vec{DG} = \frac{1}{3}\vec{DA}$ can now be expressed in terms of $\mathbf{a}$ and $\mathbf{b}$. (iii) $\vec{OG}$ is found by forming the vector addition in triangle OGD. (iv) $\vec{PA}$ is written in terms of $\mathbf{a}$ and $\mathbf{b}$ using vector addition in triangle PEA. A quadrilateral is a parallelogram if one pair of its sides is equal and parallel, i.e. two equal vectors are required. In this case it can be seen that $\vec{PA} = \vec{OG}$ making $OGAP$ a parallelogram.

Student answers

A student's answer to question 30 is now reproduced.

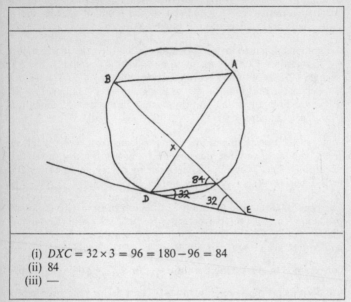

(i) $DXC = 32 \times 3 = 96 = 180 - 96 = 84$
(ii) 84
(iii) —

This type of poor quality answer is not uncommon. The diagram is useless and there is no attempt to back up the answers with any explanation. (i) The tangent and radius property has been overlooked. It has been assumed that DCE is an isoceles triangle and that DC is the bisector of angle XDC. Notice the incorrect statement that $96 = 180 - 96$, another fairly common error. (ii) The answer suggests that the student assumed that BA is parallel to DC.

Common errors

Geometry is not a popular topic with many students and examiners express surprise at the poor showing in questions which are really quite straightforward. Candidates tend to sit and look at the diagram hopefully, unable to apply any of the theorems required. To improve the chances of success read through the information given in the question and mark it on the diagram, e.g. if two angles or lines are given as equal, label them clearly on the diagram. Follow this by listing any theorem which might be relevant. In question 30, for example, the theorems used in the solution are listed in the method. They are all theorems which should spring to mind in this type of question, but many candidates missed the fact that a radius and the tangent at the point of contact are at right angles and they could not make any calculations.

A common habit is to invent or assume false properties in a diagram, e.g. in question 30 AB is assumed parallel to CD, making $y = 84°$; triangle CDE is assumed to be isosceles and angle $CDE = 32°$; X is taken as the midpoint of AO, or angle x suddenly appears as $45°$. These are all incorrect assumptions and will receive no recognition from the examiners.

Many of the questions require numerical answers. Once again, no credit can be given for an incorrect answer if there is no explanation to back it up. This is best done by referring to the theorems used. Question 30 is a typical example.

Most candidates found question 31 difficult. In similar triangles the problem is to select the correct sides to form the ratios. Remember that in similar figures corresponding sides appear opposite equal angles. E.g. in the figure on p. 39 angle $APX = $ angle ABY, $\therefore AX$ corresponds to AY, giving the ratio $\dfrac{AX}{AY}$ or $AX:AY$ (be prepared to use both forms of expressing ratios). There is also the problem of calculating the ratio of the areas of similar figures. E.g. in the same figure it has been established that in triangles APX and ABY the sides are in the ratio $1:3$, $\therefore$ the areas of the triangles are in the ratio $1:9$ and not $1:3$ as often appears. See the reference to this in the method for question 31.

Transformation geometry questions often involve graph work and will suffer accordingly unless the graphs are properly presented. Definitions of the basic transformations are not well known, in particular shear and stretch, which appear in questions 33 and 41 respectively. The product of the transformations $RM(x, y)$, as in question 32, is often carried out in the wrong order. Remember to work from right to left. Apply M to (x, y) and follow this by applying R to the image. In contrast to this process notice how in question 41 the first transformation is applied to triangle ABC and the second one is also applied to triangle ABC and not to its image. This is not a case of 'followed by' and the two examples are often confused.

In general the idea of a vector is not fully understood. The notation is not fully appreciated and many guesses have to be made. In figure (a) on page 44 OA refers to the length of the line OA. It is called a scalar quantity. $\vec{OA}$ or $\mathbf{a}$, a vector quantity, represents the length of $\vec{OA}$ (the magnitude of the vector) and the direction in which the line is pointing. Note the use of the unit vectors as in question 35 and the column vector in question 36 – the examiners complained that candidates did not understand the notation and made guesses such as $\frac{2}{5} + \frac{-3}{-1} = -2\frac{3}{5}$, which is, of course, completely irrelevant.

Question 37 is an example of the use of vectors to prove a geometrical property and those candidates who attempt this kind of question usually miss the final deduction. If two vectors are equal, e.g. $\vec{PA} = \vec{OG}$, then it can be assumed that PA is both equal and parallel to OG, enough evidence to show that $OGAP$ is a parallelogram. An extension of this idea is as follows: Suppose that $\vec{XY} = 2(\mathbf{a} + 2\mathbf{b})$ and $\vec{PQ} = (\mathbf{a} + 2\mathbf{b})$ i.e. $\vec{XY} = 2\vec{PQ}$. This tells us that XY is parallel to PQ and twice its length. If further $\vec{YZ} = k(\mathbf{a} + 2\mathbf{b})$ where k is a constant, then XY and YZ are parallel, but Y is a common point to both lines, therefore X, Y and Z are on the same straight line.

Matrices

38.

(i) $A = \begin{pmatrix} 3 & 4 & 5 \\ 2 & 6 & 4 \end{pmatrix}$ $C = \begin{pmatrix} 9 \\ 8 \end{pmatrix}$ and $AB = C$.

What is the number of rows and columns of the matrix B?

(ii) If $M = \begin{pmatrix} 4 & 3 \\ 5 & 2 \end{pmatrix}$ $N = \begin{pmatrix} 2 & 5 \\ 1 & 6 \end{pmatrix}$ and $P = 2M + N'$, *find the value of P.*

Model answer

(i) $\begin{pmatrix} 3 & 4 & 5 \\ 2 & 6 & 4 \end{pmatrix} \begin{pmatrix} \\ \\ \end{pmatrix} = \begin{pmatrix} 9 \\ 8 \end{pmatrix}$

B has 3 rows and 1 column.

(ii) $P = 2M + N' = \begin{pmatrix} 8 & 6 \\ 10 & 4 \end{pmatrix} + \begin{pmatrix} 2 & 1 \\ 5 & 6 \end{pmatrix}$

$\therefore P = \begin{pmatrix} 10 & 7 \\ 15 & 10 \end{pmatrix}$

Method (i) Write out $AB = C$ in matrix form leaving empty brackets for B. For matrix multiplication to be possible B must have three rows to match the three columns of A and one column so that AB produces the single column matrix C. (ii) To find $2M$ or $2 \times M$ double each element of M. N' the transpose of N is formed by interchanging the rows and columns of N. Add the two results to find P.

39.

If $A = \begin{pmatrix} 1 & 2 \\ 3 & 4 \end{pmatrix}$ and $B = \begin{pmatrix} 1 & 2 \\ 3 & 1 \end{pmatrix}$ *determine* AB, $3(A+B)$, A^{-1}, AA^{-1}.
Find B^2 and $2B + kI$ where k is a number and I is the unit matrix. Determine k so that $B^2 = 2B + kI$.

(Southern Universities Joint Board)

Model answer

$AB = \begin{pmatrix} 1 & 2 \\ 3 & 4 \end{pmatrix} \begin{pmatrix} 1 & 2 \\ 3 & 1 \end{pmatrix} = \begin{pmatrix} 1+6 & 2+2 \\ 3+12 & 6+4 \end{pmatrix}$

$$\therefore AB = \begin{pmatrix} 7 & 4 \\ 15 & 10 \end{pmatrix}$$

$$A + B = \begin{pmatrix} 1 & 2 \\ 3 & 4 \end{pmatrix} + \begin{pmatrix} 1 & 2 \\ 3 & 1 \end{pmatrix} = \begin{pmatrix} 2 & 4 \\ 6 & 5 \end{pmatrix}$$

$$\therefore 3(A+B) = \begin{pmatrix} 6 & 12 \\ 18 & 15 \end{pmatrix}$$

A^{-1} Determinant $= 1 \times 4 - 2 \times 3 = 4 - 6 = -2$

$$\therefore A^{-1} = -\frac{1}{2}\begin{pmatrix} 4 & -2 \\ -3 & 1 \end{pmatrix}$$

$$AA^{-1} = -\frac{1}{2}\begin{pmatrix} 1 & 2 \\ 3 & 4 \end{pmatrix}\begin{pmatrix} 4 & -2 \\ -3 & 1 \end{pmatrix} = -\frac{1}{2}\begin{pmatrix} -2 & 0 \\ 0 & -2 \end{pmatrix}$$

$$\therefore AA^{-1} = \begin{pmatrix} 1 & 0 \\ 0 & 1 \end{pmatrix}$$

$$B^2 = \begin{pmatrix} 1 & 2 \\ 3 & 1 \end{pmatrix}\begin{pmatrix} 1 & 2 \\ 3 & 1 \end{pmatrix} = \begin{pmatrix} 1+6 & 2+2 \\ 3+3 & 6+1 \end{pmatrix} \qquad B^2 = \begin{pmatrix} 7 & 4 \\ 6 & 7 \end{pmatrix}$$

$$2B + kI = 2\begin{pmatrix} 1 & 2 \\ 3 & 1 \end{pmatrix} + k\begin{pmatrix} 1 & 0 \\ 0 & 1 \end{pmatrix} = \begin{pmatrix} 2 & 4 \\ 6 & 2 \end{pmatrix} + \begin{pmatrix} k & 0 \\ 0 & k \end{pmatrix}$$

$$\therefore 2B + kI = \begin{pmatrix} 2+k & 4 \\ 6 & 2+k \end{pmatrix}$$

$$B^2 = 2B + kI \begin{pmatrix} 7 & 4 \\ 6 & 7 \end{pmatrix} = \begin{pmatrix} 2+k & 4 \\ 6 & 2+k \end{pmatrix}$$

$\Leftrightarrow 7 = 2 + k$
$\Leftrightarrow k = 5.$

Method This question tests the basic operations of matrices quite thoroughly. To find AB write down each step. Do not attempt too much mental arithmetic. For $3(A+B)$, add the corresponding elements of A and B and multiply the result by 3. To find the inverse A^{-1} of A (i) interchange the top left and bottom right elements; (ii) change the signs of the top right and bottom left elements; (iii) divide this result by the determinant of A. By definition $AA^{-1} = I$ the unit matrix, but take the opportunity to check the accuracy of A^{-1} by working out AA^{-1}. B^2 is found by evaluating $B \times B$. Use the 2×2 form of the unit matrix $I = \begin{pmatrix} 1 & 0 \\ 0 & 1 \end{pmatrix}$ to find $2B + kI$. By equating B^2 and $2B + kI$ it can be seen that they are identical if $7 = 2 + k$, i.e. $k = 5$.

40. M *and* N *are two towns to the north of a river and* X *and* Y *are bridges. There are three different roads from* M *to* Y *and one from* N *to* Y. *From* M *to* X *there are two roads and from* N *to* X *three. Record this information in the matrix form.*

$$\begin{array}{c} \\ M \\ N \end{array} \begin{array}{c} X \cdot Y \\ \begin{pmatrix} * & * \\ * & * \end{pmatrix} \end{array} \quad \textit{Let this be matrix } A.$$

R *and* S *are two towns to the south of the river. Interpret the matrix*

$$\begin{array}{c} \\ X \\ Y \end{array} \begin{array}{c} R \quad S \\ \begin{pmatrix} 2 & 3 \\ 1 & 2 \end{pmatrix} \end{array} \quad \textit{Let this be matrix B.}$$

Calculate the product AB *of the matrices. How many possible routes are there from* M *to* S *and from* N *to* R? *Briefly, justify your answers.*

(Southern Universities Joint Board)

Model answers

$$A = \begin{array}{c} \\ M \\ N \end{array} \begin{array}{c} X \quad Y \\ \begin{pmatrix} 2 & 3 \\ 3 & 1 \end{pmatrix} \end{array}$$

From bridge X there are 2 routes to town R and 3 to town S. From bridge Y there is 1 route to town R and 2 to town S.

$$AB = \begin{pmatrix} 2 & 3 \\ 3 & 1 \end{pmatrix} \begin{pmatrix} 2 & 3 \\ 1 & 2 \end{pmatrix} = \begin{pmatrix} 4+3 & 6+6 \\ 6+1 & 9+2 \end{pmatrix} = \begin{pmatrix} 7 & 12 \\ 7 & 11 \end{pmatrix}$$

There are 12 routes from M to S.
There are 7 routes from N to R.
The total number of routes from M to S comprises
$(M \to X$ then $X \to S) + (M \to Y$ then $Y \to S)$.
This total is represented by the top right element of the product AB.
The total number of routes from N to R comprises
$(N \to X$ then $X \to R) + (N \to Y$ then $Y \to R)$.
This total is represented by the bottom left element of AB.

Method A is completed from the information given in the question, e.g. there are 2 routes from M to X, $\therefore$ a 2 appears in row M column X of the matrix. Conversely it can be deduced from B

that there are 2 routes from X to R, etc. The product AB calculates the total number of routes $M \rightarrow S$, $M \rightarrow R$, $N \rightarrow S$, $N \rightarrow R$ and the candidate is asked to show some evidence that he appreciates this fact.

41. *On squared paper plot the triangle ABC with vertices $A(1,0)$ $B(5,0)$ $C(2,2)$. Label the triangle R.*

(i) R is mapped onto triangle S by means of the matrix $P = \begin{pmatrix} 0 & -1 \\ 1 & 0 \end{pmatrix}$

Plot and label the triangle S.

(ii) R is mapped onto triangle T by the matrix $Q = \begin{pmatrix} 1 & 0 \\ 0 & 3 \end{pmatrix}$

Plot and label the triangle T.
(iii) Describe geometrically the transformations P and Q.
(iv) Write down the inverse P^{-1} of matrix P and state the image of triangle S when transformed by the matrix P^{-1}.
(v) Calculate the matrix QP^{-1} and find the image of S when transformed by the matrix QP^{-1}.

Model answer

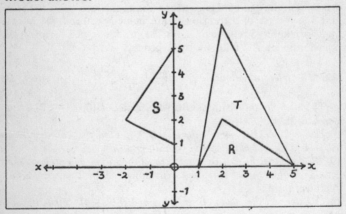

(i) $\begin{pmatrix} 0 & -1 \\ 1 & 0 \end{pmatrix} \begin{pmatrix} 1 & 5 & 2 \\ 0 & 0 & 2 \end{pmatrix} = \begin{pmatrix} 0 & 0 & -2 \\ 1 & 5 & 2 \end{pmatrix}$ triangle S.

(ii) $\begin{pmatrix} 1 & 0 \\ 0 & 3 \end{pmatrix} \begin{pmatrix} 1 & 5 & 2 \\ 0 & 0 & 2 \end{pmatrix} = \begin{pmatrix} 1 & 5 & 2 \\ 0 & 0 & 6 \end{pmatrix}$ triangle T.

(iii) P is a rotation of $90°$ anticlockwise about the point $(0,0)$. Q is a stretch of 2 units parallel to the y axis.

(iv) The determinant of $P = 0 - (-1) = +1$

the inverse $P^{-1} = \begin{pmatrix} 0 & 1 \\ -1 & 0 \end{pmatrix}$

The image of S under P^{-1} is the triangle R.

(v) $QP^{-1} = \begin{pmatrix} 1 & 0 \\ 0 & 3 \end{pmatrix} \begin{pmatrix} 0 & 1 \\ -1 & 0 \end{pmatrix} = \begin{pmatrix} 0 & 1 \\ -3 & 0 \end{pmatrix}$

$\begin{pmatrix} 0 & 1 \\ -3 & 0 \end{pmatrix} \begin{pmatrix} 0 & 0 & -2 \\ 1 & 5 & 2 \end{pmatrix} = \begin{pmatrix} 1 & 5 & 2 \\ 0 & 0 & 6 \end{pmatrix}$

The image of S under QP^{-1} is triangle T.

Method Prepare the graph and plot the triangle R. (i) Write the coordinates of A, B and C as column matrices and pre-multiply each by P to obtain the triangle S. This can be condensed by writing the three columns in the form of a 2×3 matrix as shown. Read the coordinates of S as $(0, 1)$ $(0, 5)$ and $(-2, 2)$. (ii) Apply Q to triangle R (not its image S). Plot triangles S and T and label them, as in the figure on page 45, to obtain the result (iii). (iv) Note that the inverse of a transformation matrix performs the inverse transformation: S returns to R. (v) The product QP^{-1} performs the transformation P^{-1} followed by Q, hence $S \to T$.

42. *The transformation* $T : \begin{pmatrix} x \\ y \end{pmatrix} \to \begin{pmatrix} 2 & 4 \\ 0 & 2 \end{pmatrix} \begin{pmatrix} x \\ y \end{pmatrix}$ *is given. On*

graph paper plot the square OABC with vertices $O(0, 0)$ $A(2, 0)$ $B(2, 2)$ and $C(0, 2)$.
(i) Under T, OABC maps onto $OA_1 B_1 C_1$. Find the coordinates of $A_1 B_1$ and C_1 and plot them on your diagram.
(ii) T is equivalent to two single transformations, one followed by another. Define them clearly and write down the 2×2 matrices which represent them.
(iii) Under T the point P maps onto $P_1(7, -4)$. Find the co-ordinate of P.

Model answer

(i) $\begin{pmatrix} 2 & 4 \\ 0 & 2 \end{pmatrix} \begin{pmatrix} 2 & 2 & 0 \\ 0 & 2 & 2 \end{pmatrix} = \begin{pmatrix} 4 & 12 & 8 \\ 0 & 4 & 4 \end{pmatrix}$

A is $(4, 0)$; B is $(12, 4)$; C is $(8, 4)$.
(ii) An enlargement of scale factor 2 with centre $(0, 0)$ followed by a shear parallel to the x axis.

The enlargement has matrix $\begin{pmatrix} 2 & 0 \\ 0 & 2 \end{pmatrix}$, the shear $\begin{pmatrix} 1 & 2 \\ 0 & 1 \end{pmatrix}$.

(iii) $\begin{pmatrix} 2 & 4 \\ 0 & 2 \end{pmatrix}\begin{pmatrix} x \\ y \end{pmatrix} = \begin{pmatrix} 7 \\ -4 \end{pmatrix}$

$\Rightarrow 2x + 4y = 7$

$\quad\quad 2y = -4 \Leftrightarrow y = -2$

$\Rightarrow 2x + 4(-2) = 7$

$\Leftrightarrow 2x - 8 = 7$

$\Leftrightarrow 2x = 8 + 7 \Leftrightarrow 2x = 15 \Leftrightarrow x = 7 \cdot 5$

P is the point $(7 \cdot 5, -2)$.

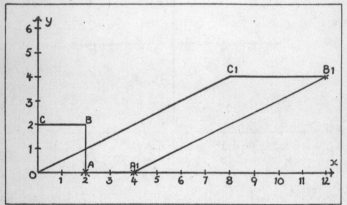

Method Prepare the graph and plot the square $OABC$. (i) Carry out the transformation T on A, B and C as shown in question 41 and plot the points $A_1 B_1 C_1$. (ii) It is necessary to see from the diagram that there is an enlargement followed by a shear, or vice versa. (iii) Knowing that the matrix $\begin{pmatrix} 2 & 0 \\ 0 & 2 \end{pmatrix}$ gives an enlargement of scale factor 2 in $(0,0)$ it is possible to deduce the matrix for the shear. (iii) To find P let its coordinates be (x, y). Set up the equations produced by T and solve them.

43. (i) M and N are transformations of the plane and are defined by $M : \begin{pmatrix} x \\ y \end{pmatrix} \rightarrow \begin{pmatrix} y \\ x \end{pmatrix}$ $N : \begin{pmatrix} x \\ y \end{pmatrix} \rightarrow \begin{pmatrix} -x \\ -y \end{pmatrix}$. Illustrate on a diagram the points $P(4,1)$ and $Q(5,4)$, their images P_1 and Q_1, P_2 and Q_2 under M and N respectively. Describe the transformations carefully and state the matrices M and N which give them. Evaluate MN and define the product of the transformations MN as a single transformation.

(ii) Find a 2 × 2 transformation matrix which will map (3, − 5) onto (4, 2) and (1, 4) onto (7, 12).

Model answer

(i) $P(4, 1)$, $Q(5, 4)$, $P_1(1, 4)$, $Q_1(4, 5)$, $P_2(-4, -1)$, $Q_2(-5, -4)$.

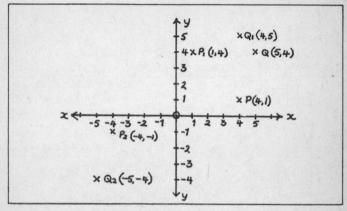

M is a reflection in the straight line $y = x$.
N is a rotation of $180°$ about the point $(0, 0)$.

$$M = \begin{pmatrix} 0 & 1 \\ 1 & 0 \end{pmatrix} \quad N = \begin{pmatrix} -1 & 0 \\ 0 & -1 \end{pmatrix}$$

$$MN = \begin{pmatrix} 0 & 1 \\ 1 & 0 \end{pmatrix} \begin{pmatrix} -1 & 0 \\ 0 & -1 \end{pmatrix} \begin{pmatrix} x \\ y \end{pmatrix}$$

$$= \begin{pmatrix} 0 & -1 \\ -1 & 0 \end{pmatrix} \begin{pmatrix} x \\ y \end{pmatrix} = \begin{pmatrix} -y \\ -x \end{pmatrix}$$

MN is equivalent to a reflection in the straight line $y = -x$.

(ii) Let the matrix be $\begin{pmatrix} a & b \\ c & d \end{pmatrix}$

Then $\begin{pmatrix} a & b \\ c & d \end{pmatrix} \begin{pmatrix} 3 \\ -5 \end{pmatrix} = \begin{pmatrix} 4 \\ 2 \end{pmatrix}$ and $\begin{pmatrix} a & b \\ c & d \end{pmatrix} \begin{pmatrix} 1 \\ 4 \end{pmatrix} = \begin{pmatrix} 7 \\ 12 \end{pmatrix}$

$\Leftrightarrow 3a - 5b = 4$ $\Leftrightarrow a + 4b = 7$
$ 3c - 5d = 2$ $ c + 4d = 12$

$ 3a - 5b = 4$ $ 3c - 5d = 2$
$ a + 4b = 7$ $ c + 4d = 12$

$$\Leftrightarrow 3a - 5b = 4$$
$$3a + 12b = 21$$
$$\Leftrightarrow -17b = -17$$
$$\Leftrightarrow b = 1$$
$$\Leftrightarrow a + 4 = 7$$
$$\Leftrightarrow a = 3$$

$$\Leftrightarrow 3c - 5d = 2$$
$$3c + 12d = 36$$
$$\Leftrightarrow -17d = -34$$
$$\Leftrightarrow d = 2$$
$$\Leftrightarrow c + 8 = 12$$
$$\Leftrightarrow c = 4$$

The required matrix is $\begin{pmatrix} 3 & 1 \\ 4 & 2 \end{pmatrix}$.

Method (i) The diagram, which should be drawn on graph paper, helps the candidate to recognise the transformations M and N, but he should know that a reflection in the line $y = x$ causes $(x, y) \rightarrow (y, x)$, and a rotation of $180°$ changes the signs of the coordinates. Starting with the identity matrix $I = \begin{pmatrix} 1 & 0 \\ 0 & 1 \end{pmatrix}$, M and N can be deduced as follows: $\begin{pmatrix} 0 & 1 \\ 1 & 0 \end{pmatrix}$ interchanges the x and y values, $\begin{pmatrix} -1 & 0 \\ 0 & -1 \end{pmatrix}$ changes the signs. Evaluate the product MN, in that order, and transform (x, y). The result $(-y, -x)$ is a reflection in the line $y = -x$. (ii) It is not possible to anticipate any of the elements of the required matrix here, so let the elements be a, b, c, and d, form the simultaneous equations and solve them.

Student answers

A student's answer to question 40 is now reproduced.

(i) $\begin{pmatrix} 0 & -1 \\ 1 & 0 \end{pmatrix} \begin{pmatrix} 1 \\ 0 \end{pmatrix} = \begin{pmatrix} 0 \\ 1 \end{pmatrix} \begin{pmatrix} 0 & -1 \\ 1 & 0 \end{pmatrix} \begin{pmatrix} 5 \\ 0 \end{pmatrix}$

$= \begin{pmatrix} 0 \\ 5 \end{pmatrix} \begin{pmatrix} 0 & -1 \\ 1 & 0 \end{pmatrix} \begin{pmatrix} 2 \\ 2 \end{pmatrix} = \begin{pmatrix} -2 \\ 2 \end{pmatrix}$

(ii) $\begin{pmatrix} 1 & 0 \\ 0 & 3 \end{pmatrix} \begin{pmatrix} 0 \\ 1 \end{pmatrix} = \begin{pmatrix} 0 \\ 3 \end{pmatrix} \begin{pmatrix} 1 & 0 \\ 0 & 3 \end{pmatrix} \begin{pmatrix} 0 \\ 5 \end{pmatrix}$

$= \begin{pmatrix} 0 \\ 15 \end{pmatrix} \begin{pmatrix} 1 & 0 \\ 0 & 3 \end{pmatrix} \begin{pmatrix} -2 \\ 2 \end{pmatrix} = \begin{pmatrix} -2 \\ 6 \end{pmatrix}$

(iii) P is an anticlockwise rotation.
Q —

(iv) $P^{-1} = \begin{pmatrix} 0 & 1 \\ -1 & 0 \end{pmatrix}$

$$\begin{pmatrix} 0 & 1 \\ -1 & 1 \end{pmatrix}\begin{pmatrix} 0 \\ 1 \end{pmatrix} = \begin{pmatrix} 1 \\ 0 \end{pmatrix}\begin{pmatrix} 0 & 1 \\ -1 & 0 \end{pmatrix}\begin{pmatrix} 5 \\ 0 \end{pmatrix}$$

$$= \begin{pmatrix} -5 \\ 0 \end{pmatrix}\begin{pmatrix} 0 & 1 \\ -1 & 0 \end{pmatrix}\begin{pmatrix} -2 \\ 2 \end{pmatrix} = \begin{pmatrix} 2 \\ 2 \end{pmatrix}$$

(v)

(i) The transformation P has been carried out correctly, but in (ii) the transformation Q has been applied to the triangle S and not triangle R as instructed, $\therefore$ triangle T is incorrect. (iii) The centre and angle of rotation for P have been omitted and as the scales on the x and y axes are different it would be more difficult to recognise the transformation Q even if it was correct. (iv) The inverse of P is correct, probably with some luck, because the determinant of P is 1, so there is no knowing whether this candidate remembered the determinant stage. He did not see that the inverse matrix returns S to R and in making the calculations wrote $(5, 0)$ for $(0, 5)$, producing a point which would not fit on the graph. From here he lost the thread of the question and was unable to attempt (v).

Common errors

Matrix manipulation is usually quite good as long as all the elements are numbers, but when they are letters take care of the basic algebra. The main confusion occurs over the permissibility of operations. E.g. if $A = (1 \quad 2)$ $B = \begin{pmatrix} 3 \\ 4 \end{pmatrix}$ $C = \begin{pmatrix} 4 & 7 \\ 3 & 2 \end{pmatrix}$ $D = \begin{pmatrix} 5 & 2 \\ 1 & 4 \end{pmatrix}$, the values of $C \pm D$ can be evaluated but $A \pm C$, $B \pm C$, $B \pm A$ cannot. The matrices involved in addition and subtraction must have the same order. CD and DC can both be evaluated but produce different results, whereas CA, DA, BC and BD cannot even be evaluated, although AC, AD, CB and DB are possible to work out. Remember that in general $AB \neq BA$, the main exceptions involving the unit and inverse matrices, i.e. $A \times I = I \times A = A$ and $A \times A^{-1} = A^{-1} \times A = I$. Pay special attention to the product BA. It is nearly always considered impossible but $\begin{pmatrix} 3 \\ 4 \end{pmatrix}(1 \quad 2) = \begin{pmatrix} 3 & 6 \\ 4 & 8 \end{pmatrix}$ is the correct calculation.

Note the calculation of the inverse matrix in question 39. It is common to forget to divide by the determinant of the matrix.

Students fail to appreciate how the basic transformation matrices work. In $\begin{pmatrix} 0 & 1 \\ -1 & 0 \end{pmatrix}\begin{pmatrix} x \\ y \end{pmatrix} = \begin{pmatrix} y \\ -x \end{pmatrix}$, the matrix $\begin{pmatrix} 0 & 1 \\ -1 & 0 \end{pmatrix}$ has the effect of changing (x, y) to $(y, -x)$, a rotation of 90° clockwise about $(0, 0)$. There are 6 more of these basic matrices – the reflections in the x and y axes and the lines $y = \pm x$, and the rotations about $(0, 0)$ of 90° anticlockwise and 180°. It is worthwhile learning them.

A common error in the above procedure is to attempt it as $(x, y)\begin{pmatrix} 0 & 1 \\ -1 & 0 \end{pmatrix} = (-y, x)$. The calculation is possible but produces incorrect coordinates. Always write the coordinates as a column matrix and pre-multiply it by the transformation matrix.

Arithmetic and statistics

Arithmetic

44. (a) *Correct each of the following numbers to* (i) *three significant figures;* (ii) *three decimal places.*
36·3783   0·0083263   846·054
(b) *The speed of light is* 3×10^8 *m/s. Find in standard form* (i) *how far it travels in km in 1 hour;* (ii) *how long it takes to tavel* $4·5 \times 10^8$ *km.*

Model answer

(a) Number   (i) significant figures (ii) decimal places
    36·3783   36·4   36·378
    0·0083263   0·00833   0·008
    846·054   846   846·054

(b) (i) distance in 1 hour $= 3 \times 10^8 \times 60 \times 60$ m
$$= 3 \times 36 \times 10^{10} \text{ m}$$
$$= 108 \times 10^{10} \text{ m}$$
$$= 1·08 \times 10^{12} \text{ m}$$
$$= 1·08 \times 10^{12} \div 10^3 \text{ k m}$$

    the required distance $= 1·08 \times 10^9$ km.

(ii) Time $= \dfrac{\text{distance}}{\text{speed}} = \dfrac{4·5 \times 10^8 \times 10^3}{3 \times 10^8}$ second s

$$= 1·5 \times 10^3 \text{ seconds}$$

$$= \frac{1·5 \times 10^3}{60} \text{ minutes} = \frac{150}{6} \text{ minutes}$$

    the required time $= 25$ minutes.

Method (a) Distinguish clearly between the significant figure and decimal place answers. Notice in particular how 0·0083263 becomes 0·00833 to three significant figures. The zeros before the 8 are not significant. (b) To change m/s to km/hr first change to m/hr by multiplying by 60×60. Now change the m/hr to km/hr by dividing by 10^3, keeping the results in standard form as much as possible. (ii) Working in m/s units, which seem to be easier here, divide the distance expressed in m by the speed in m/s.

45. *A circle of radius* 20 *cm has a sector of angle* 72° *cut from it. This is folded and fixed to form a cone, so that the curved arc of the circumference forms the base of the cone.*
(a) *Calculate* (i) *the curved area of the cone;* (ii) *the radius of the*

base of the cone.

(b) The cone is inverted and filled with sugar which has a mass of 900 g per 1000 cm³. Calculate the mass of the sugar in the cone. Give your answers to 2 significant figures. Take π as 3·14.

Model answer

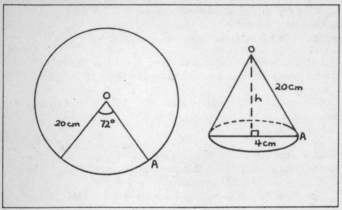

(a) (i) Area of sector $= \dfrac{72}{360} \times \pi \times 20 \times 20 \text{ cm}^3$

$$= \pi \times 4 \times 20 \text{ cm}^3$$

$$= 80\pi \text{ cm}^3$$

the curved area of the cone $= 251 \cdot 2 \text{ cm}^2$ or 250 cm^2

(ii) The curved area $= \pi r l = 80\pi$

$$\pi \times r \times 20 = 80\pi$$

$$\Leftrightarrow r = \dfrac{80 \times \pi}{20 \times \pi}$$

the base radius $= 4 \cdot 0 \text{ cm}$.

(b) Volume of cone $= \frac{1}{3}\pi r^2 h$

$h = \sqrt{(20^2 - 4^2)} = \sqrt{(400 - 16)} = \sqrt{384} = 19 \cdot 6 \text{ cm}$

Mass of sugar $= \dfrac{1}{3} \times \pi \times 4 \times 4 \times 19 \cdot 6 \times \dfrac{9}{10}$

$$= 3 \cdot 14 \times 16 \times 19 \cdot 6 \times 0 \cdot 3$$

$$= 295 \cdot 4 \text{ g or } 300 \text{ g to 2 significant figures.}$$

Method A diagram like the one above will help to make the question clearer. (a) (i) Calculate the area of the sector, which is $\frac{72}{360}$ or $\frac{1}{5}$ of the area of the circle. (ii) The radius OA of the circle becomes the slant height of the cone. If πrl, the area of the curved surface is equated to 80π, the π cancels and r is calculated easily. (b) In order to find the volume of the cone its vertical height is found by using the theorem of Pythagoras. To find the mass of sugar multiply the expression for the volume by $\frac{9}{10}$. There is no need to calculate the volume separately. Notice that each answer is expressed to 2 significant figures as requested.

46. (i) *The mass of a liquid is given as* $0\cdot87$ *g per* cm^3. *Find the greatest possible error in calculating the mass of* 2 *litres of the liquid.*
(ii) *The model of a car has a scale of* $1:20$. *The fuel tank of the actual car holds* 40 *litres of petrol. What is the capacity of the fuel tank of the model?*

Model answer
(i) the greatest mass $= 0\cdot875$ g, the least mass $= 0\cdot865$ g
    the greatest possible error per $cm^3 = 0\cdot005$ g
    the greatest error in finding 2 litres $= 0\cdot005 \times 2000$ g
$$= 10 \text{ g}.$$
(ii) 40 litres $= 40 \times 1000$ cm^3
$$\text{capacity of model tank} = \frac{40 \times 1000}{20 \times 20 \times 20}$$

$$= 5 \text{ cm}^3$$

Method (i) No measurement is exact, so $0\cdot87$ g given to two significant figures can lie between $0\cdot875$ and $0\cdot865$ grammes, i.e. $0\cdot87 \pm 0\cdot005$ g. Multiply $0\cdot005$ g, the greatest possible error, by 2000 which is 2 litres expressed in cm^3. (ii) This is another test in the ratios of similar figures. The corresponding measurements have a ratio $1:20$, $\therefore$ the volumes are in the ratio $1:20^3$. Hence the volume of the tank is divided by $20 \times 20 \times 20$.

47. (i) *An alloy consists of* 3 *metals A, B and C. The ratio* $A:B = 4:7$, $B:C = 9:10$. *Find the ratio* $A:C$.
(ii) *The scale of a map is* $1:50\,000$, *and* 1 *hectare is the area of a square with side* 100 *m. Find the area represented on the map if the area on the ground is* 120 *hectares.*

Model answer
(i) $\dfrac{A}{B} = \dfrac{4}{7}$ $\qquad\qquad\qquad$ $\dfrac{C}{B} = \dfrac{10}{9}$

$$\Leftrightarrow A = \frac{4}{7}B \text{ and } C = \frac{10}{9}B$$

$$\therefore \frac{A}{C} = \frac{4}{7}B \div \frac{10}{9}B = \frac{4B}{7} \times \frac{9}{10B} = \frac{18}{35}$$

the ratio $A : C = 18 : 35$.

(ii) 120 hectares $= 120 \times 100 \times 100$ m^2

the area on the map $= \dfrac{12 \times 10^5}{50\,000 \times 50\,000}$ m^2

$$= \frac{12 \times 10^5}{25 \times 10^8} = \frac{12}{25 \times 10^3} \text{ m}^2$$

$$= \frac{12 \times 100 \times 100}{25 \times 10^3} \text{ cm}^2 = \frac{48 \times 10}{100} = 4 \cdot 8$$

The area on the map $= 4 \cdot 8$ cm^2.

Method (i) Work in fractions to find A in terms of B and C in terms of B. In the ratio $A : C$ expressed as a fraction B cancels leaving the numerical answer $A : C = 18 : 35$. (ii) Notice that the area on the ground is divided by the square of $50\,000$ and m^2 are multiplied by the square of 100 to obtain cm^2. With so many zeros, work in the form 10^n where possible and notice the trick of putting $\frac{12}{25} = \frac{48}{100}$ to minimise the calculations.

48. $x = 0 \cdot 030y$. Then x is:

(A) 30% of y   (B) 0·3% of y
(C) 0·03% of y   (D) 3% of y

(D) is the correct answer.

Method $1\% = \frac{1}{100} = 0 \cdot 01$
$\therefore 0 \cdot 030$ or $0 \cdot 03 = 3\%$ giving D as the correct answer. This multiple choice question tests the candidate's ability to convert % to decimal. Remember that 1% is 0·01 as a decimal.

49. (i) *A report comparing the export of cars from the UK to France in a given year with that of the previous year showed that the number exported had increased by 12%, but that the average price per car in £ had increased by 20%. Calculate the percentage increase of the total value of cars exported to France. (ii) In the same year the value of the £ fell against the French franc by 14%. Find the increase or decrease per cent in the total value of the exports in francs.*

Model answer

(i) In the previous year let n = number of cars, £p = price of each.

the new number = $\dfrac{112}{100}n$ the new price = $\dfrac{£120}{100}p$

The previous value = £ np new value = $\dfrac{£112}{100} \times \dfrac{120}{100}np$

$= \dfrac{1344}{1000}np = £1{\cdot}344\,np$

∴ The increase in value = $1{\cdot}344\,np - 1\,np = £0{\cdot}344\,np$
the % increase = 34·4.

(ii) the new value = £1·344 np

∴ the new value in francs = $1{\cdot}344\,np \times \dfrac{86}{100} = 1{\cdot}1558\,np$

there is an increase of $1{\cdot}1558\,np - 1\,np = 0{\cdot}1558\,np$
∴ the increase in francs is 15·58%.

Method To increase or decrease a number by $r\%$ multiply it by
$\dfrac{100+r}{100}$ or $\dfrac{100-r}{100}$ respectively.

(i) There are no actual sums of money mentioned in the question so use letters to represent the number and price of the cars. Increase these accordingly, using the above formula. The difference between the new and old value gives the increase in the value in decimal form. Using again the fact that $0{\cdot}01 = 1\%$, the % increase is obtained.
(ii) Let the quantity np now represent the previous value in francs. Use the above formula to reduce it by 14%. By comparing this with the original it is clear that there is an increase of $0{\cdot}1558\,np$ francs, which is the equivalent of 15·58%.

50. (i) *The rateable value of a house is £150. Rates are raised at 52p in the £1. The house is given a new rateable value of £200 but the actual bill for the rates remains the same as before. At how many pence in the £1 is the new rate levied?* (ii) *A householder can pay his quarterly gas bill using one of two tariffs as follows:*

	General	Gold
standing charge	£1·25	£5·50
charge per therm	21·6p	14·1p

He uses 60 therms in a quarter. Which tariff will be cheaper and by how much?

How many therms must he use in a quarter for the bills to be the same? Give your answer to one decimal place.

Model answer

(i) Let the new rate be x p in the £1.
The original rate bill = 150×52p
$$200x = 150 \times 52$$
$$\Leftrightarrow x = \frac{150 \times 52}{200} = \frac{15 \times 26}{10}$$

∴ the new rate is 39p in the £1.

(ii) General tariff

	£	
standing charges =	1·25	21·6
60 therms at 21·6p =	12·96	6
Total	14·21	129·6

Gold tariff

	£	
standing charge =	5·50	14·1
60 therms at 14·1 =	8·46	6
Total	13·96	84·6

∴ the gold tariff is cheaper by 25p.

Let x = the number of therms used.
On general tariff the bill = $125 + 21·6x$ pence
On gold tariff the bill = $550 + 14·1x$ pence.
∴ $125 + 21·6x = 550 + 14·1x$
$\Leftrightarrow 21·6x - 14·1x = 550 - 125$
$\Leftrightarrow 7·5x = 425$
$$\Leftrightarrow x = \frac{425}{7·5} = 56·667$$

The bills are equal if 56·7 therms are used.

Method Questions concerning everyday arithmetic must be expected, without explanation of the specific terms given, e.g. tariff, rateable value. (i) Let x pence be the unknown rate. Form an equation and solve for x. (ii) Set the solution as a bill and the cheaper tariff can easily be calculated. To obtain the last answer let x be the unknown number of therms. Form expressions for the cost under both tariffs, remembering to work in the same units. Equate the two expressions and solve for x. At the last stage an error can easily occur. The recurring decimal 0·666... is 0·7 to 1 decimal place.

Statistics

51. *The histogram in the figure below shows the results of an experiment involving the length in cm of a root vegetable. Find the mode, mean and median lengths of the vegetables.*

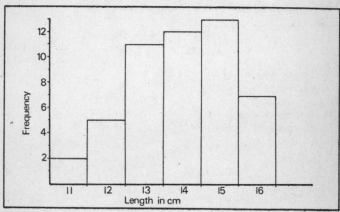

Model answer

Length in cm	frequency	product
11	2	22
12	5	60
13	11	143
14	12	168
15	13	195
16	7	112
Totals	50	700

The mode is 15 cm.
The mean is $700 \div 50 = 14$ cm.
The median is the $\frac{1}{2}(50+1)$th number, i.e. the $25\frac{1}{2}$th
$2+5+11 = 18$, $18+12 = 30$
The median is 14 cm.

Method To find the three averages construct the frequency table from the histogram. The mode is the class with the greatest frequency.

The mean is calculated from $\dfrac{\text{sum of the class} \times \text{frequencies}}{\text{sum of the frequencies}}$. Construct the product column to the right of the frequencies. The median, the middle root when they are lined up in order of length, is located by adding the frequencies to see that the $25\frac{1}{2}$th root occurs in the class containing 12 roots, i.e. 14 cm.

52. *Calculate the value of x in the frequency table, given that the mean is 6·6 calculated from the mid-interval values.*

Class	1–3	4–6	7–9	10–12
frequency	3	x	15	2

Model answer

Class	mid-interval	frequency	product
1– 3	2	3	6
4– 6	5	x	$5x$
7– 9	8	15	120
10–12	11	2	22
Totals		$20+x$	$148+5x$

$$\frac{148+5x}{20+x} = 6\cdot6$$

$$\Leftrightarrow 148+5x = 6\cdot6(20+x)$$
$$\Leftrightarrow 148+5x = 132+6\cdot6x$$
$$\Leftrightarrow 148-132 = 6\cdot6x-5x$$
$$\Leftrightarrow 16 = 1\cdot6x$$
$$\Leftrightarrow x = 10.$$

Method First write the table in column form. The mean is calculated using the mid-interval values when the classes are grouped. Follow the steps shown in question 51. This produces an equation in x which is solved in the usual way.

53. *The lifetime in hours, to the nearest half hour, of 500 electric light bulbs is given in the frequency distribution below.*

Life (hr)	200–	400–	600–	800–	1000–	1200–	1400–	1600–1800
frequency	10	50	70	130	100	80	40	20

Draw a cumulative frequency graph and use it to estimate (i) the median; (ii) the semi-interquartile range; (iii) the percentage of the bulbs which have a life of 900 hr or more.

Model answer

life (hr)	frequency	cumulative frequency
200–	10	10
400–	50	60
600–	70	130
800–	130	260
1000–	100	360
1200–	80	440
1400–	40	480
1600–1800	20	500

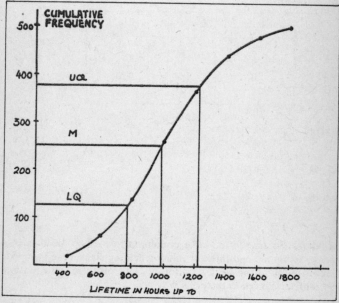

(i) the median is the 250th bulb: its life = 990 hr.

(ii) the UQ is the 375th bulb: its life = 1240 hr;
    the LQ is the 125th bulb: its life = 790 hr;
    the semi-interquartile range: = 450 ÷ 2 = 225 hr.

(iii) 192 bulbs have a life of up to 900 hr
    the number with a life of 900 hr or more = 500 − 192 = 308

the $\% = \dfrac{308}{500} = \dfrac{616}{1000} = 61 \cdot 6$

$61 \cdot 6\%$ have a life of 900 hr or more.

Method Draw up the cumulative frequency column to the right of the frequencies. Construct the cumulative frequency graph using as large a scale as possible. The numbers on the horizontal scale should be the upper limits of the classes, in this case $399\frac{1}{2}$, $599\frac{1}{2}$ hr, etc., but it will suffice to use 400, 600 hr, etc., with the wording 'lifetime in hours up to ...' (i) The median bulb is the 250th (ignoring the $\frac{1}{2}$ with a large sample). Draw the horizontal line through 250 and read off the lifetime below, as in the figure on page 68. (ii) Similarly use the 125th and 375th bulbs as the lower and upper quartiles respectively. The semi-interquartile range is half the difference between the upper and lower quartiles. (iv) From the graph 192 bulbs have a life of up to 900 hr. Count from the 193rd up to the 500th, i.e. 308.

54. *Red, white and blue tickets are sold for a raffle which only has one prize. The probability that a red ticket will win the prize is $\frac{1}{5}$ and the probability that a white ticket will win is $\frac{3}{4}$. The probability that the winning ticket is blue is:*
(A) $\frac{3}{20}$ (B) $\frac{1}{20}$ (C) $\frac{17}{20}$ (D) $\frac{5}{9}$.

(B) is the correct answer.

Method This is a question involving total probability. A red, a white **or** a blue can win, not a red **and** a white, etc. Note that the separate probabilities are added. The probability that a red or a white will win is: $\frac{1}{5} + \frac{3}{4} = \frac{4}{20} + \frac{15}{20} = \frac{19}{20}$.

The probability of a blue win $= 1 - \frac{19}{20} = \frac{1}{20}$, since it is a certainty (1) that a red or a white or a blue will win.

55. *The probability that A attends school on a particular day is $\frac{5}{6}$. The probability that B attends school on the same day is $\frac{9}{10}$. Find the probability that :*
(i) both A and B attend school on that day;
(ii) only A attends school on that day;
(iii) only one of them attends on that day;
(iv) neither attends on that day.

Model answer
  (i) The probability that both attend $= \frac{5}{6} \times \frac{9}{10} = \frac{45}{60} = \frac{3}{4}$
  (ii) The probability that A and not B attends $= \frac{5}{6} \times \frac{1}{10} = \frac{1}{12}$
  (iii) The probability that B and not A attends $= \frac{1}{6} \times \frac{9}{10} = \frac{3}{20}$

the probability that only one attends $= \frac{5}{60} + \frac{9}{60} = \frac{14}{60} = \frac{7}{30}$

(iv) The probability that neither attends $= \frac{1}{6} \times \frac{1}{10} = \frac{1}{60}$.

Method This question mainly involves compound probability. (i) A **and** B can both attend. Multiply the probabilities. (ii) The probability that B does not attend is $1 - \frac{9}{10} = \frac{1}{10}$. (iii) Total probability is involved here if A and not B **or** B and not A attends, $\therefore$ the two probabilities are added. (iv) The product of the non-events is required here. Notice that the sum of (i), (ii) and (iv) is 1. These are all the possible events that can happen.

Student answers

A student's answers to question 47 and 54 are now reproduced.

---

47. (i) $A : C = 4 : 10$

(ii) $\text{Area} = \dfrac{120 \times 100}{50000} = \dfrac{12}{50} = 0 \cdot 24$

$\text{Area} = 2 \cdot 4 \times 10^{-1}$

(i) The student has picked out the numbers corresponding to the letters A and C in the given ratios, taking no account of how B compares with A and C. (ii) He has twice failed to apply the square of the dimension when converting an area. He has also omitted the units in the answer.

54. The student ringed the answer C, suggesting that he evaluated $1 - (\frac{1}{5} \times \frac{3}{4})$, i.e. he multiplied the probabilities where he should have added.

Common errors

Arithmetical accuracy is essential to all mathematics. At one time logarithms were the only aid to making calculations easier. More recently the slide rule has been accepted and now the electronic calculator is permitted in some examinations. However, it is still essential to be able to make accurate calculations 'manually', to be able to round off correctly to the required number of significant figures or decimal places and to manipulate fractions properly. Trigonometry, similar triangles, percentage and probability all involve fraction and ratio work, so that if the student's work with fractions is weak all of these topics will be suspect.

It is surprising how many candidates will make $\frac{1}{2}+\frac{1}{3}=\frac{2}{5}$ where it should be $\frac{3}{6}+\frac{2}{6}=\frac{5}{6}$. This error occurs particularly in probability work where they momentarily forget the basic rules. Others are unable to work out $\frac{4}{75}\times 100$; $5\frac{2}{3}$ is written as $5\cdot 66$ to two decimal places instead of $5\cdot 67$; $3\frac{1}{3}$ hr, expressed as $3\cdot 33$ hr, becomes 3 hr 33 minutes where it should be 3 hr 20 minutes. The following example of careless approximation occurs frequently: $\sqrt{122\cdot 6}=\sqrt{120}=11\cdot 0$ – where it should, of course, read $\sqrt{122\cdot 6}=\sqrt{123}=11\cdot 1$. Remember to select the correct square root.

Questions about arithmetic in everyday life are often poorly answered because of a failure to recognise the terms 'rateable value', 'tax allowance', 'tariff', etc. Logarithms and slide rules are used, wrongly, to work out sums of money. Remember that bills and taxes require exact amounts of money, while logarithms and slide rules give only approximate answers. These sums must be worked out 'long hand' or by electronic calculator.

Usually the numbers involved in a question have been arranged to work out conveniently, e.g. $37\pi + 63\pi = 100\pi = 314$, but many candidates work out $37\times\pi$ and $63\times\pi$ and then add the two results. The extra calculation increases the chance of an error. Others resort to logarithms to work out 4×25 and, unfortunately, even $4+25$!

Conversion of units in the metric system is often rather weak. Note the pattern of the following correct conversions: to convert cm to m divided by 100, cm^2 to m^2 divide by 100^2, cm^3 to m^3 divide by 100^3. Conversely, to convert m to cm multiply by 100, etc. It is worth spending some time familiarising yourself with these.

In statistics there are a number of terms which must be recognised if the questions are to be attempted successfully. The mean, mode and median are often confused. Students do not always understand frequency distribution and quartiles. In question 51 the mean is often calculated as (sum of classes) ÷ (sum of frequencies) where it should be (sum of class × frequencies) ÷ (sum of frequencies) and the mode is given as 13, its frequency, instead of as 15 cm, the length.

Statistical graphs are often poorly presented. If this occurs in the case of question 53, it will not be possible to give good readings for the median, etc. Remember that the markings on the horizontal axes must be numbers which represent the upper class limits, i.e.

the largest possible number in that class.

The answers to probability questions are often guessed at incorrectly, many of the answers offered being greater than 1. Remember that if the probabilities of an event occurring and not occurring are p and q respectively then $p + q = 1$. Lastly take care of the fraction work here – it so often spoils some good attempts.

Trigonometry and calculus

Trigonometry

56. *In the diagram triangle ABC has AB = 10 cm, DC = 8 cm and angle ABD = 52°. AD is perpendicular to BC. Calculate to two significant figures (i) the length AD; (ii) the length BD; (iii) the length AC and (iv) angle ACD.*

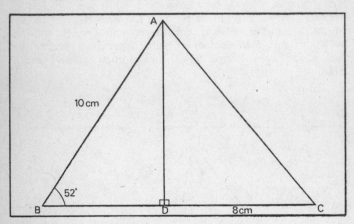

Model answer

(i) In triangle ABD $\dfrac{\text{opposite}}{\text{hypotenuse}} = \dfrac{AD}{10} = \sin 52°$

$$\Leftrightarrow AD = 10 \times \sin 52°$$

$$= 10 \times 0·788$$

$AD = 7·88$ or $7·9$ cm.

(ii) In triangle ABD $\dfrac{\text{adjacent}}{\text{hypotenuse}} = \dfrac{BD}{10} = \cos 52°$

$$\Leftrightarrow BD = 10 \times \cos 52°$$

$$= 10 \times 0·616$$

$BD = 6·16$ or $6·2$ cm.

(iii) In triange ADC $AC^2 = 8^2 + 7·88^2$

$$= 64 + 62·1 = 126·1$$

$\therefore AC = 11·2$ or 11 cm.

(iv) In triangle ADC $\dfrac{\text{opposite}}{\text{adjacent}} = \dfrac{7\cdot88}{8} = 0\cdot985 = \tan C$

angle $C = 44\cdot6°$.

Method Three-figure tables are used in all of the trigonometry questions. (i) and (ii) AD and BD are found in triangle ABD in which side AB and angle ABD are known. Determine the positions of the sides relative to the angle of 52°, i.e. opposite, adjacent and hypotenuse. Determine the ratios to be used, stating them clearly. Find the ratios from the natural sine, etc., tables and calculate the lengths as shown. (iii) In triangle ADC the sides AD and DC are known, $\therefore$ use the theorem of Pythagoras to find AC. (iv) The two known sides form the tangent ratio. Express it as a three-figure decimal and find the angle with this ratio in the natural tangent table.

57.

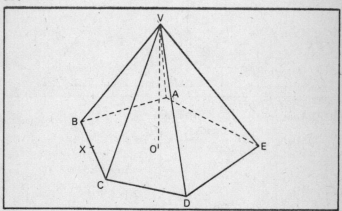

The diagram shows a right pyramid with a regular pentagon $ABCDE$ as its base, V is the vertex and O the centre of the base. The vertical height $VO = 8$ cm and $BO = 10$ cm. X is the midpoint of BC. Calculate
  (i) the length of the slant edge VB;
 (ii) the angle between VB and the base;
(iii) the length OX;
(iv) the angle between the slant face VBC and the base.

Model answer

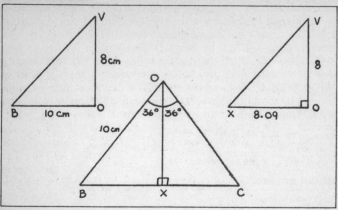

(i) in triangle VBO $VB^2 = 8^2 + 10^2$

$$= 64 + 100 = 164$$

$$\therefore VB = 12{\cdot}8 \text{ cm.}$$

(ii) The required angle is VBO.

In triangle VBO $\dfrac{\text{opposite}}{\text{adjacent}} = \tan VBO = \dfrac{8}{10} = 0{\cdot}800$

the angle between VB and the base $= 38{\cdot}7°$.

(iii) In triangle BOX, angle $BOX = \frac{1}{2}(360° \div 5) = 36°$

$$\dfrac{\text{adjacent}}{\text{hypotenuse}} = \dfrac{OX}{10} = \cos 36°$$

$$\Leftrightarrow OX = 10 \times \cos 36°$$

$$= 10 \times 0{\cdot}809$$

$$\therefore OX = 8{\cdot}09 \text{ cm.}$$

(iv) The required angle is VXO.

In triangle VXO $\dfrac{\text{opposite}}{\text{adjacent}} = \tan XVO = \dfrac{8{\cdot}09}{8} = 1{\cdot}01$

angle $XVO = 45{\cdot}3°$

angle $V\,XO = 90° - 45{\cdot}3° = 44{\cdot}7°$

Method In this three-dimensional question several triangles will be required. Draw them separately, as in the figure on page 75, and label in all the known information. (i) *VB* can be calculated using the theorem of Pythagoras in triangle *VBO*. (ii) Name the required angle. See how it can be calculated from triangle *VBO*. (iii) *OX* is perpendicular to *BC*, triangle *BOC* is an isosceles triangle with angle *BOC* = 72°, from the regular pentagon, ∴ *OX* can now be found in triangle *BOX*. (iv) Using this value of *OX* it is possible to find angle *VXO* in triangle *VXO*. Notice that it is easier to calculate 8·09 ÷ 8 than 8 ÷ 8·09, ∴ the angle *XVO* can be calculated and subtracted from 90° to give angle *VXO*.

58.   *Given that* $\sin 30° = \frac{1}{2}$, *without using tables find the values of* (i) *sin* 60° + *cos* 60°; (ii) *sin* 150° + *cos* 150°; (iii) *sin* 240° − *cos* 330°, *leaving any* $\sqrt{\ }$ *signs in your answer*.

Model answer

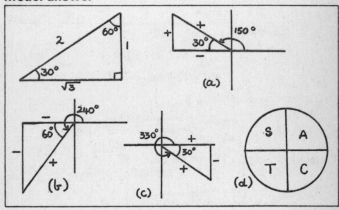

(i) $\cos 60° = \frac{1}{2}$: $\sin 60° = \frac{\sqrt{3}}{2}$: $\cos 30° = \frac{\sqrt{3}}{2}$

$$\sin 60° + \cos 60° = \frac{\sqrt{3}}{2} + \frac{1}{2} = \frac{\sqrt{3}+1}{2}.$$

(ii) $\sin 150° + \cos 150° = \sin 30° - \cos 30°$

$$= \frac{1}{2} - \frac{\sqrt{3}}{2} = \frac{1-\sqrt{3}}{2}.$$

(iii) $\sin 240° - \cos 330° = -\sin 60° - \cos 30°$

$$= -\frac{\sqrt{3}}{2} - \frac{\sqrt{3}}{2} = -\sqrt{3}.$$

Method Draw the 30° : 60° : 90° triangle and complete the ratios sin 60°, cos 60° and cos 30°. (i) can now easily be completed by putting the two fractions over one denominator. (ii) Draw the small sketch as in figure (a) on page 76, showing that $\sin 150° = + \sin 30°$ and $\cos 150° = - \cos 30°$. (iii) Draw the small sketches (b) and (c) showing that $\sin 240° = - \sin 60°$ and $\cos 330° = + \cos 30°$. The fractions are simplified in each case. The additional sketch in figure (d) with the initials A, S, T, C confirms the quadrants in which **A**ll ratios, **S**in, **T**an and **C**os, are positive.

59. *A is the point on the Earth's surface at the position 10°N 50°W. B is the point at the position 60°S 50°W. C is on the same parallel of latitude as B and 1100 km due east of B. Calculate (i) the distance from A to B on the Earth's surface; (ii) the position of C. Take $\pi = \frac{22}{7}$ and the Earth's radius as 6372 km.*

Model answer

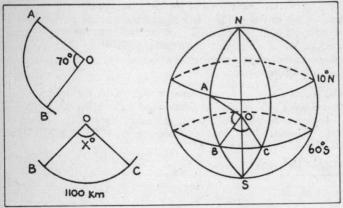

(i) The circumference of the Earth $= 2 \times \pi \times 6372$ km

$$\frac{AB}{2 \times \pi \times 6372} = \frac{70}{360}$$

$$\Leftrightarrow AB = \frac{2 \times 22 \times 6372 \times 70}{7 \times 360} = \frac{44 \times 708}{4} = 11 \times 708 \text{ km}$$

∴ the distance between A and $B = 7788$ km.

(ii) Circumference of latitude 60°S $= 2 \times \pi \times 6372 \cos 60°$

$$= 2 \times \pi \times 6372 \times 0.5$$

$$= 6372\pi \text{ km}$$

$$\frac{X°}{360°} = \frac{1100}{6372\pi}$$

$$\Leftrightarrow X° = \frac{360 \times 1100 \times 7}{6372 \times 22} = \frac{40 \times 100 \times 7}{708 \times 2} = \frac{3500}{177}$$

$X° = 19\cdot8$
C is at longitude $50° - 19\cdot8° = 30\cdot2°$W.
The position of C is $60°$S $30\cdot2°$W.

Method Start this question by drawing a figure of the Earth as a sphere, marking in the points A, B and C clearly. (i) AB is the arc of a great circle (its radius is that of the Earth), subtending an angle of $10° + 60° = 70°$ at the centre of the Earth. Use the relationship: $\dfrac{\text{length of arc}}{\text{circumference}} = \dfrac{\text{angle subtended at centre}}{360°}$ to calculate the length AB. The resulting fraction cancels conveniently with the help of π taken as $\frac{22}{7}$. (ii) The radius of the circle of latitude $A°$ north or south = the radius of the Earth $\times \cos A°$, hence the circumference of the circle $60°$S is $2 \times \pi \times 6372 \cos 60°$. Now use the above ratios to calculate $X°$. Subtract $X°$ from the $50°$W to find the new longitude. Note that the two small sketches of arcs AB and BC help to clarify the problem.

60. *B and C are two points on a straight road, the bearing of C from B being 060°. B and C are 200 m apart. From B a tree is sighted on a bearing of 040° and from C the same tree is on a bearing of 290°. Calculate (i) the distance of the tree from B; (ii) the shortest distance from the tree to the road.*

Model answer

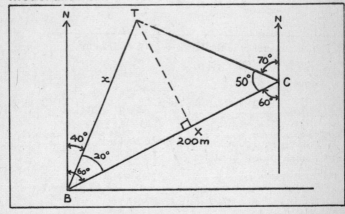

(i)

In triangle BTC $\dfrac{x}{\sin 50°} = \dfrac{200}{\sin BTC}$

angle $BTC = 180° - 70° = 110°$ $\sin 110° = \sin 70°$

$$x = \frac{200 \sin 50°}{\sin 70°} = \frac{200 \times 0·766}{0·940}$$

The distance from the tree to B is 163 m.

(ii) The required distance is TX.

In triangle TXB $\dfrac{TX}{163} = \sin 20°$

$\Leftrightarrow TX = 163 \times \sin 20°$

$= 163 \times 0·342 = 55·7$ m.

The shortest distance from T to $BC = 55·7$ m.

Method Draw a diagram like the one on p. 78, the main problem being to obtain as many angles as possible in the triangle from the given bearings. Remember that a bearing of 060° means 'Look north and turn clockwise through 60°'. From this information angles TBC and TCB can be found.

(i) It can be seen that there is no right angle in triangle BTC, but as two angles and one side are known the sine rule can be applied to find TB. Note how the sine of an obtuse angle is dealt with.

(ii) The shortest distance between a point and a line is the perpendicular drawn from the point to the line, hence use right-angled triangle trigonometry in triangle TXB to find TX.

Calculus

61. (i) *Calculate the gradient at the point $P(2, -16)$ on the curve $y = x^3 - 2x^2 - 8x$. Find the equation of the tangent at P.*

(ii) *Find the rate of change of y with respect to x at the point $(0,0)$ on the same curve.*

(iii) *The figure shows the graph of $y = (x-1)(x-3); \; 0 \leqslant x \leqslant 3$. Calculate the total area of the shaded region.*

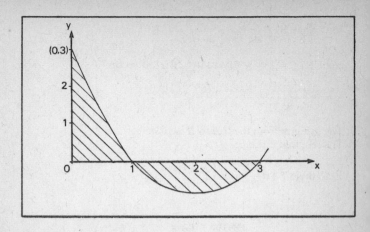

Model answer

(i) $y = x^3 - 2x^2 - 8x$

$$\frac{dy}{dx} = 3x^2 - 4x - 8$$

∴ the gradient at $P(2, -16) = 12 - 8 - 8 = -4$.
The tangent at P will be $y = -4x + c$.
It passes through $(2, -16)$. $-16 = -8 + c \Rightarrow c = -8$.
The equation of the tangent at P is $y = -4x - 8$.

(ii) The $\frac{dy}{dx}$ at $(0, 0)$ is -8

i.e. the rate of change of y with respect to x at 0 is -8.

(iii) $y = x^2 - 3x - x + 3 = x^2 - 4x + 3$

The total area $= \displaystyle\int_0^1 y\, dx + \int_1^3 v\, dx$

$$\int_0^1 (x^2 - 4x + 3)\, dx = \left[\frac{x^3}{3} - 2x^2 + 3x \right]_0^1$$

$= (\tfrac{1}{3} - 2 + 3) - 0 = 1\tfrac{1}{3} \text{ units}^2$

$$\int_1^3 y\, dx = \left(\frac{27}{3} - 18 + 9 \right) - 1\tfrac{1}{3} = -1\tfrac{1}{3}$$

Total area shaded $= 2 \times 1\tfrac{1}{3} = 2\tfrac{2}{3} \text{ units}^2$.

Method (i) Calculate the $\dfrac{dy}{dx}$ at $x = 2$ to give the gradient at P.

Use the straight line form $y = mx + c$ where m is the gradient. Find the value of c by substituting $(2, -16)$ in $y = mx + c$. (ii) The gradient measures the rate of change of y with respect to x. (iii) To find the area integrate between the limits given. In this case the brackets must be multiplied out first. The total area is obtained by adding the areas between $0 - 1$ and $1 - 3$. Notice that the latter is negative (the area is below the x axis), but this is ignored when finding the total area.

62. *A particle moves in a straight line such that its velocity v metres per second is given after time t seconds by the equation $v = 6 + 5t - t^2$. Calculate :*
(i) the time when the particle is at rest instantaneously;
(ii) the initial velocity;
(iii) the acceleration after 1·5 seconds;
(iv) the maximum velocity.

(Welsh Joint Education Committee)

Model answer
(i) $v = 0 \Leftrightarrow 6 + 5t - t^2 = 0$ or $t^2 - 5t - 6 = 0$

$$\Leftrightarrow (t - 6)(t + 1) = 0 \Leftrightarrow t = +6 \quad \text{or} \quad -1$$

∴ the particle is at rest when $t = 6$ seconds.
(ii) The initial velocity $(t = 0)$ is 6 m/s

(iii) the acceleration $\dfrac{dv}{dt} = 5 - 2t$

when $t = 1·5$, the acceleration $= 5 - 3 = 2$ m/s^2.

(iv) For maximum velocity $\dfrac{dv}{dt} = 0 \Leftrightarrow 5 - 2t = 0$

$\Leftrightarrow 2t = 5 \Rightarrow t = 2·5$ seconds.
The maximum velocity $= 6 + 5 \times 2·5 - 2·5^2 = 6 + 12·5 - 6·25$.
The maximum velocity $= 12·25$ m/s.

Method (i) Solve the quadratic and select only the positive values of t. (ii) The initial velocity requires $t = 0$. (iii) acceleration is the rate of change of velocity with respect to time, i.e. it is necessary to differentiate velocity to find acceleration. (iv) The maximum point on the velocity/time graph occurs where its gradient is 0, i.e. where the acceleration is zero.

63. *A solid rectangular block has a square base of side x cm and a vertical height h cm.*

(i) Find expressions for the volume V cm³ and the total surface area A cm² of the block, in terms of x and h.

(ii) Use your results in (i) to show that if the volume of the block is 8 litres, then $A = \dfrac{3 \cdot 2 \times 10^4}{x} + 2x^2.$

(iii) Find $\dfrac{dA}{dx}$ *and the value of x which makes A a minimum.*

(iv) Show that when A is a minimum the box is a cube.

(The Associated Examining Board)

Model answer

(i) length $= x$ cm : breadth $= x$ cm : height $= h$ cm
   $V = x^2 h : A = 2x^2 + 4xh.$

(ii) 8 litres $= 8 \times 10^3$ cm³

$$\therefore 8 \times 10^3 = x^2 h \Rightarrow h = \frac{8 \times 10^3}{x^2}$$

$$A = \frac{4x \times 8 \times 10^3}{x^2} + 2x^2 \therefore A = \frac{3 \cdot 2 \times 10^4}{x} + 2x^2$$

(iii)
$$A = 3 \cdot 2 \times 10^4 x^{-1} + 2x^2 \quad \text{and} \quad \frac{dA}{dx} = -3 \cdot 2 \times 10^4 x^{-2} + 4x$$

$$\frac{dA}{dx} = 0 \text{ for a minimum} \Rightarrow \frac{-3 \cdot 2 \times 10^4}{x^2} + 4x = 0$$

$$\Leftrightarrow 4x^3 - 3 \cdot 2 \times 10^4 = 0 \Leftrightarrow 4x^3 = 3 \cdot 2 \times 10^4$$

$$\Leftrightarrow x^3 = 0 \cdot 8 \times 10^4$$

$$\Leftrightarrow x^3 = 8 \times 10^3 \Leftrightarrow x = 2 \times 10 = 20 \text{ cm}$$

A is a minimum when $x = 20$ cm.

(iv) When $x = 20$ $V = 8000 = 400$ $h \Leftrightarrow h = 20$ cm, the box is a cube of $20 \times 20 \times 20$ cm³.

Method (i) Express the volume and area in terms of x and h. (ii) The instruction is to write A in terms of x only. To do this eliminate h by putting it in terms of V and x from the volume formula, where V is now 8×10^3 cm³. (iii) Now differentiate A with respect to x, put the result equal to 0 and solve the resulting equation to find x, which gives the minimum area. Notice how the algebra and arithmetic work out conveniently when no errors are made. (iv) By letting $x = 20$ in the volume formula, h is also found to be 20 cm, therefore the box is a cube.

Student answers

A student's answer to question 57 is now reproduced.

(i) $BV = \sqrt{8^2 + 10^2}$

$= \sqrt{64 + 100} = \sqrt{164} \quad BV = 12 \cdot 8$

(ii) $\dfrac{x}{10} = \sin 36 = 0 \cdot 588$

$\Leftrightarrow x = 5 \cdot 88 \, \text{cm}$

$\text{Cos} \, x = \dfrac{5 \cdot 88}{12 \cdot 8} \doteqdot 0 \cdot 46 \, (SR)$

$x = 62 \cdot 6°$

(iii) $\dfrac{x}{10} = \cos 36 = 0 \cdot 809$

$x = 8 \cdot 09 \, \text{cm}$

(iv) $\tan x = \dfrac{8}{10} \doteqdot 0 \cdot 8$

$x = 38 \cdot 7°$

The student used the diagram printed on the examination paper and did not make a copy on the answer sheet. He has used the letter x for all the unknowns, which makes the working difficult to follow. He knows the basic trigonometrical ratios but is unable to apply them in three dimensions. (i) has been calculated correctly but the units have been omitted from the answer. (ii) is incorrect because the angle VBX has been calculated as the angle between V and the base instead of angle VBO. (iii) is correct but in (iv), again, the incorrect angle VBO has been used to represent the angle between the face VBC and the base. The correct angle is VXO.

Common errors

The greatest possible error is to enter the examination without a sound knowledge of the three ratios. Most of the examinations contain a fairly straightforward question involving ratios in right-angled triangles and the marks gained are usually good.

Errors do occur in calculations, often as a result of poor reading of the slide rule. These errors can produce absurd answers which should be spotted immediately, e.g. in question 56(ii), when with $AB = 10$ cm and $DC = 8$ cm it is unlikely that BD will measure 62 cm. This error is only a slip of the decimal point, but it could be avoided with some thought about the range in which sensible answers may lie.

In (iii) of the same question, when using the theorem of Pythagoras, errors occur in the selection of the square root $-\sqrt{126}$ appears as $3 \cdot 55$ or $35 \cdot 5$ where it should be $11 \cdot 2$.

Remember, too, that there are two square roots associated with any number but only one of them is relevant at the time, e.g. $\sqrt{4 \cdot 0} = 2$ and $\sqrt{40} = 6 \cdot 33$.

Some Boards include the sine and cosine rules in their syllabi, and often these rules are used in a question which can be reduced to sine, cosine and tangent ratios in right-angled triangles, which is usually a simpler method.

Three-dimensional problems require good diagrams. It is not easy to give a three-dimensional effect but practice will improve the results. It helps to represent lines which are not visible as broken lines, as in the figure on page 74.

Sketches of individual triangles to be used will also help to pinpoint any difficulties.

If the answer is to be a bearing it must be given in the correct form, which is now a three-figure angle, such as $060°$ or $153°$, etc.

In calculus questions there is a tendency to lapse into integration when trying to differentiate and vice versa. Differentiation of terms with negative powers such as $\dfrac{1}{x^2}$ is rarely done correctly. Write it as x^{-2} which becomes $-2x^{-3}$ when differentiated and $\dfrac{x^{-1}}{-1}$ when integrated.

In the application of calculus to distance, velocity and acceleration, there is some confusion over which process to use. If the distance $s = f(t)$ then the velocity v is obtained from the $\dfrac{ds}{dt}$, and the acceleration from $\dfrac{d^2s}{dt^2}$ i.e. $\dfrac{dv}{dt}$. Conversely if the acceleration is given as a function of t, integrate to find the velocity and integrate again to find the distance. Do not forget the integration constant each time $(+C)$.

The Examination Paper

To conclude this book a sample of one half of a typical O-level paper is presented with a student's answers followed by model answers to his questions.

Assume that the time allotted for the sample is $1\frac{1}{4}$ hr, 30 minutes for section A and 40 minutes for section B, and use the time left over to check your working.

The sample has a maximum mark of 50, section A carrying 30 marks and section B 20 marks.

MATHEMATICS I

Instructions to candidates Attempt all questions in section A and any two questions from section B. All essential working must be shown with the answers.

Section A

1. A man sells a car for £630 which is a loss of 16% on what he paid for it. How much did he pay for the car?

2. Express 21 m^2 in cm^2, giving your answer in standard form.

3. Find the real solutions of the equation $x^2 - 3x = 54$.

4. Copy the frequency distribution and from the histogram fill in the frequencies.

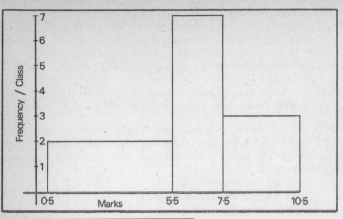

Marks	1–5	6–7	8–10
Frequency			

5. The universal set is whole numbers. Find the solution set of $21 < 3x + 5 \leqslant 41$.

6. A circle is drawn with its centre at the point $(10, 0)$ and a radius of 8 units. Calculate the length of the tangent to the circle which is drawn from the point $(-7, 0)$.

7. If $p = \dfrac{x}{a} + b$, express a in terms of p, x and b.

8. (i) Find the gradient of the straight line $3x - 4y = 5$.
   (ii) Find the coordinates of the point where the same line cuts the y axis.

9. In a triangle XYZ a line AB is drawn parallel to XY cutting XZ at A and YZ at B so that $AB = 6$ cm, $YB = 10$ cm and $BZ = 5$ cm. Calculate
 (i) the length of XY;
 (ii) the ratio of the areas of triangles ABZ to XYZ.

10. A is an obtuse angle and $\sin A° = \frac{4}{5}$. Without using tables evaluate $2 - \tan A°$.

Section B

11. A survey in a group of people shows that 48 have a colour TV. 20 have a black-and-white TV and 6 have neither. The probability

that a person chosen at random has a colour TV is $\frac{2}{3}$.

(a) (i) How many people are there in the group?
   (ii) Draw a Venn diagram to show the information.
   (iii) How many have a colour and a black-and-white TV?

(b) Find the probability that a person chosen at random has
   (i) a colour TV only;
   (ii) a colour and a black-and-white TV;
   (iii) either colour or black-and-white TV, but not both.

12. A ship leaves a port A at noon travelling at 16 km/hr on a bearing 035°. At 1430 hr it changes course and travels at the same speed on a bearing 160° until 1500 hr when it reaches a point B. Calculate to the nearest metre
   (i) the distance that B is east of A;
   (ii) the distance that B is north of A;
   (iii) the bearing of A from B.

13. The matrix shows the number of ice creams and ice lollies with their prices sold by a shop over a period of time.

	Price (p)		
	8	12	15
lollies	20	10	5
ice cream	15	8	6

Denote this matrix by M.

 (i) Write down a matrix A which when multiplied by M will give the money taken on lollies and ice creams separately.
 (ii) Produce these totals.
 (iii) Write down a matrix B which when multiplied by M gives the separate totals of the number of lollies and ice creams sold.
 (iv) Write down a matrix C which when multiplied with M will give the total number of lollies and ice creams sold at each price.
 (v) Multiply your answer to (ii) by C. What does this answer represent?

Specify the order of multiplication in each case.

Student answers

1.
$$630 \times \frac{16}{100} = \frac{1008}{10} = 100\cdot8$$

the cost is $630 + 100\cdot8 = £730\cdot80$

2. $21 \text{ m}^2 = 21 \times 100 = 2100 = 2.1 \times 10^3 \text{ cm}^2$

3. $\qquad x^2 - 3x = 54$

   $x^2 - 3x - 54 = 0$

   $(x-9)(x+6) = 0 \qquad x = 9$

4.

Marks	1–5	6–7	8–10
frequency	2	7	3

5. $\qquad 21 < 3x + 5 \leqslant 41$

   $x = 1 \quad 21 < 3 + 5 \leqslant 41 \qquad x = 8 \quad 21 < 24 + 5 \leqslant 41$

   $x = 2 \quad 21 < 6 + 5 \leqslant 41 \qquad x = 9 \quad 21 < 27 + 5 \leqslant 41$

   $x = 5 \quad 21 < 15 + 5 \leqslant 41 \qquad x = 10 \quad 21 < 30 + 5 \leqslant 41$

   $x = 6 \quad 21 < 18 + 5 \leqslant 41 \qquad x = 11 \quad 21 < 33 + 5 \leqslant 41$

   $x = 7 \quad 21 < 21 + 5 \leqslant 41 \qquad x = 12 \quad 21 < 36 + 5 \leqslant 41$

   $x = 6, 7, 8, 9, 10, 11, 12$

6. $x^2 = 17^2 + 8^2$

   $\qquad = 289 + 64 = 353$

   $x = 18.8$

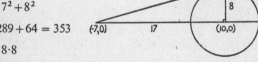

7. $p = \dfrac{x}{a} + b \qquad\qquad ap = x + b$

   $$a = \frac{x+b}{p}$$

8. (i) gradient $= \frac{4}{3}$ (ii) cuts the y axis at $(0, \frac{5}{4})$

9. $\dfrac{XY}{6} = \dfrac{10}{5} = 2$

   $XY = 12 \text{ cm}$

   (ii) triangle $XYZ : ABZ = 2:1$

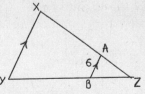

10. $\tan A = \frac{4}{3}$

$2 - 1\frac{1}{3} = \frac{2}{3}$

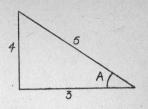

13. $M = \begin{pmatrix} 20 & 10 & 5 \\ 15 & 8 & 6 \end{pmatrix}$

(i) $A = \begin{pmatrix} 8 \\ 12 \\ 15 \end{pmatrix}$

(ii) $\begin{pmatrix} 20 & 10 & 5 \\ 15 & 8 & 6 \end{pmatrix} \begin{pmatrix} 8 \\ 12 \\ 15 \end{pmatrix} = \begin{pmatrix} 160 + 120 + 75 \\ 120 + 96 + 90 \end{pmatrix}$

$= \begin{pmatrix} 365 \\ 306 \end{pmatrix}$

lollies = £3·65   ice creams = £3·06

(iii) $(1 \ 1) \begin{pmatrix} 20 & 10 & 5 \\ 15 & 8 & 6 \end{pmatrix} = (20 + 15 \ \ 10 + 8 \ \ 5 + 6)$

$= (35 \ 18 \ 11)$

(iv) $\begin{pmatrix} 20 & 10 & 5 \\ 15 & 8 & 6 \end{pmatrix} \begin{pmatrix} 1 \\ 1 \end{pmatrix}$

11. a (i) there are $48 + 20 + 6 = 74$

(ii)

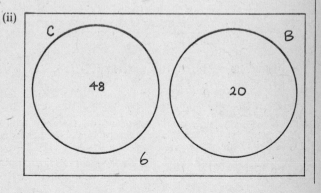

(iii) nobody has both colour TV and a black and white.
b (i) the probability that a person chosen at random has colour TV only is $\frac{2}{3}$.

Comments

This is a poor script which has not reached the pass mark. It contains many of the common errors which could be avoided with more thought and care. The mark for each answer is included at the end of each comment.

Section A (3 marks each)
1. Is incorrect because the original cost price must be taken as 100%. The £630 is 84% of the cost price. (0)
2. Standard form has been correctly interpreted, but the conversion from m^2 to cm^2 is incorrect. (1)
3. The basic working is correct, but the term 'real' has been confused with 'positive integer'. (2)
4. The point of the question has been missed. When the class intervals are uneven the fact that the frequency is proportional to the area of the block must be used. (0)
5. The method of trial and error is correct as long as the solutions are integers. Otherwise the model method is to be preferred. (3)
6. The faulty diagram has placed the right angle at the incorrect vertex. It should be between the radius and tangent. (1)
7. These questions produce most incorrect answers. When multiplied by a the expression should read $ap = x + ab$. (1)
8. These errors could have been avoided if the given equation had been rearranged into the form $y = mx + c$. (0)
9. (i) The student was impressed by the numbers 10 and 5 and missed the required ratio $YZ : BZ = 15 : 5$. (0) (ii) A further error has occurred by ignoring the rule that if the sides are in the ratio $1 : n$, the areas of similar triangles are the ratio $1 : n^2$. (0)
10. The numerical value of the ratio is correct, but the fact that the tangent of an obtuse angle is negative has been omitted. (2)

Section B (10 marks each)
13. (i) is correct. (ii) would be correct but for an arithmetic error in the ice lolly total. (iii) Unfortunately the matrix given here is the correct answer to (iv). The student has not appreciated this and has been unable to proceed further. (3)
11. It is incorrect to assume that the 48 people with colour TV have colour TV only. They include those with colour and black-

and-white. An error like this makes it impossible to score any marks.

Model answers to these questions are now given. Question 12 is solved by using right-angled triangle trigonometry. The answers are as follows: (i) 25·7 km; (ii) 25·2 km; (iii) 045·6°.

Model answers

1. Let £x be the original cost

$$x \times \frac{84}{100} = 630$$

$$\Leftrightarrow x = 630 \times \frac{100}{84} = 100 \times \frac{30}{4}$$

$\therefore$ the original cost is £750.

2. $21 \text{ m}^2 = 21 \times 100 \times 100 = 21 \times 10^4$

$\quad = 2\cdot1 \times 10^5 \text{ cm}^2.$

3. $x^2 - 3x - 54 = 0$

$\Leftrightarrow (x-9)(x+6) = 0$

$\Leftrightarrow x-9 = 0 \quad \text{or} \quad x+6 = 0 \Leftrightarrow x = 9 \quad \text{or} \quad -6.$

4.

mark	1–5	6–7	8–10
frequency	10	14	9

area of column $1-5 = 5 \times 2 = 10$

area of column $6-7 = 2 \times 7 = 14$

area of column $8-10 = 3 \times 3 = 9.$

5. $21 < 3x + 5$

$\Leftrightarrow 21 - 5 < 3x$

$\Leftrightarrow 16 < 3x \Rightarrow x > 5\frac{1}{3} \qquad x = 6, 7, 8, 9, \ldots$

$\quad 3x + 5 \leqslant 41$

$\Leftrightarrow 3x \leqslant 41 - 5$

$\Leftrightarrow 3x \leqslant 36 \Leftrightarrow x \leqslant 12 \qquad x = 12, 11, 10.$

$\therefore x \in \{6, 7, 8, 9, 10, 11, 12\}.$

6. $x^2 = 17^2 - 8^2$

   $= 289 - 64 = 225$

   The length of the tangent = 15 units.

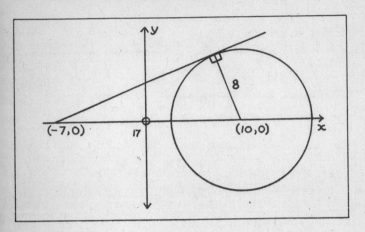

7.
$$p = \frac{x}{a} + b$$

$$\Leftrightarrow p - b = \frac{x}{a} \Leftrightarrow a = \frac{x}{p-b}$$

8. $3x - 4y = 5$

   $\Rightarrow -4y = -3x + 5$

   $\Leftrightarrow 4y = 3x - 5$

   $\Leftrightarrow y = \frac{3}{4}x - \frac{5}{4}$

   (i) The gradient is $\frac{3}{4}$; (ii) it cuts the y axis at $(0, -\frac{5}{4})$.

9. (i) Triangle XYZ is similar to ABZ

   $$\frac{XY}{AB} = \frac{YZ}{BZ} \qquad \frac{XY}{6} = \frac{10+5}{5} = \frac{3}{1}$$

   $\Leftrightarrow XY = 18$ cm.

   (ii) The sides are in the ratio $3:1$
   $\therefore$ triangle $XYZ : ABZ = 9:1$.

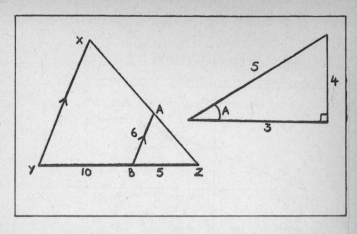

10. $\sin A° = \frac{4}{3}$ A is obtuse $\therefore \tan A = -\frac{4}{3} = -1\frac{1}{3}$
    $\therefore 2 - \tan A = 2 - (-1\frac{1}{3}) = 3\frac{1}{3}$.

13. (i) $M = \begin{pmatrix} 20 & 10 & 5 \\ 15 & 8 & 6 \end{pmatrix}$ $A = \begin{pmatrix} 8 \\ 12 \\ 15 \end{pmatrix}$ Evaluate $M \times A$

(ii) $\begin{pmatrix} 20 & 10 & 5 \\ 15 & 8 & 6 \end{pmatrix} \begin{pmatrix} 8 \\ 12 \\ 15 \end{pmatrix} = \begin{pmatrix} 160 + 120 + 75 \\ 120 + 96 + 90 \end{pmatrix} = \begin{pmatrix} 355 \\ 306 \end{pmatrix}$

money taken on lollies = £3·55; on ice creams = £3·06.

(iii) $\begin{pmatrix} 20 & 10 & 5 \\ 15 & 8 & 6 \end{pmatrix} \begin{pmatrix} 1 \\ 1 \\ 1 \end{pmatrix}$ $\therefore B = \begin{pmatrix} 1 \\ 1 \\ 1 \end{pmatrix}$.

(iv) $(1 \ 1)\begin{pmatrix} 20 & 10 & 5 \\ 15 & 8 & 6 \end{pmatrix}$ $\therefore C = (1 \ 1)$.

(v) $(1 \ 1)\begin{pmatrix} 355 \\ 306 \end{pmatrix} = (355 + 306) = (661)$

This product gives the total money taken = £6·61.

11. a (i) Let the number of people = x

$\frac{48}{x} = \frac{2}{3}$

$\Leftrightarrow 48 \times 3 = 2x \Leftrightarrow x = 24 \times 3$

There are 72 people in the group.

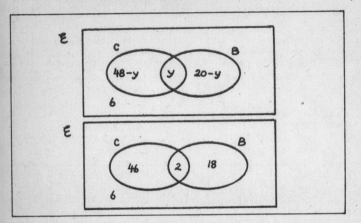

Let $n(C \cap B) = y$

$\therefore 48 - y + y + 20 - y + 6 = 72$

$\Leftrightarrow 74 - y = 72 \Leftrightarrow y = 2$

The number with colour and black-and-white TV = 2.

b (i) $\dfrac{46}{72}$ or $\dfrac{23}{36}$; (ii) $\dfrac{2}{72}$ or $\dfrac{1}{36}$; (iii) $\dfrac{46 + 18}{72}$ or $\dfrac{8}{9}$.

Other study aids in the **key facts** series

KEY FACTS CARDS

30p: Woodwork	50p: Economics
Metalwork	Elementary Mathematics
Henry IV Part I	Algebra
Henry V	Modern Mathematics
Merchant of Venice	English History
Richard II	(1815–1939)
Richard III	Chemistry
Twelfth Night	Physics
35p: Latin	Biology
Julius Caesar	Geometry
40p: New Testament	Geography
50p: German	French
Macbeth	Arithmetic and Trigonometry
Geography–Regional	General Science
English Comprehension	Additional Mathematics
English Language	Technical Drawing

KEY FACTS COURSE COMPANIONS

55p: Economics	55p: Geography
Modern Mathematics	French
Algebra	Physics
Geometry	Chemistry
Arithmetic and Trigonometry	English
Additional Mathematics	Biology

KEY FACTS A-LEVEL BOOKS

55p: Chemistry	55p: Pure Mathematics
Biology	Physics

KEY FACTS PASSBOOKS

95p: Modern Mathematics	95p: Physics
English History (1815–1939)	Geography
Biology	French
Chemistry	English

All **KEY FACTS** titles are published by

Intercontinental Book Productions
Berkshire House, Queen Street, Maidenhead, SL6 1NF
in conjunction with the distributors, Seymour Press Ltd.,
334 Brixton Road, London SW9 7AG
Prices are correct at time of going to press.